Adopted Son

The Life, Wit & Wisdom of
William Wirt, 1772-1834

William Wirt, 1772-1834

Copy of 1808 engraving of William Wirt by C.B.J. Fevret de St. Memin.
(Courtesy of The Library of Virginia.)

Adopted Son

The Life, Wit & Wisdom of William Wirt, 1772-1834

By Gregory K. Glassner

**With a Foreword
By Senator Eugene J. McCarthy**

Kurt-Ketner Publishing Co.
Madison County, Virginia

Dedicated to my mother, Kathryn Wallace Glassner

Library of Congress Catalog Card Number 97-67763

International Standard Book Number 1-57087-328-3

Printed in the United States of America
by Professional Press, Chapel Hill, NC 27515-4371

Frontispiece: William Wirt, 1808, engraving by C.B.J. Fevret de St. Memin.
(Courtesy of The Library of Virginia)

Foreword

When one reads of the early history of the United States and of the works of men like Jefferson, the Adamses, Madison, Monroe and others, he knows, or assumes, that there are persons like William Wirt, who, of lesser fame, possibly of no fame, have contributed to the work of building the nation. Greg Glassner writes of such a person in this important historical report of the life and times of William Wirt, and especially of Wirt offering himself as a third party candidate to break the early trend to confine politics to two parties, a condition which John Adams foresaw as a most serious threat to the proper political working of the Constitution.

Eugene J. McCarthy
Woodville, Virginia
(U.S. Senator, 1959-1971; Contender for 1968 Democratic Presidential Nomination; Presidential Candidate, 1976, 1988)

Acknowledgments

Few published works are the product of one person laboring alone. I would like to acknowledge my wife Hardy Glassner, for encouraging me to complete this book and for putting up with the loss of shared moments that is the legacy of any author who also has a "day job." I would also like to acknowledge the following people who contributed editing expertise and/or words of encouragement during the process: Suzanne Garofalo, Ann L. Miller, Terry Adams, Tucker Hill and Janie Matthews. I wish to thank the helpful staff of the following research facilities: The Library of Virginia, the Alderman Library of the University of Virginia, the Virginia Historical Society, Maryland Historical Society, Orange County Historical Society, Albemarle County Historical Society, Norfolk's Kirn Memorial Library, the Madison County Library, the State Library of Florida, and the Earl Gregg Swem Library at the College of William & Mary.

-- *G.K Glassner*

Preface

My knowledge of William Wirt dates back to the day I happened across a short reference to him in a guide to Charlottesville and the surrounding area. I immediately grabbed my copy of Madison County's history and discovered another reference to Wirt. It stated that William Wirt, who later became Attorney General of the United States, once lived in Madison County and started his law practice there. As Managing Editor of the *Madison County Eagle*, I sensed a story. Shortly after I began my quest for information on Wirt, however, I realized there was more of a story than I could capture in the confines of a newspaper feature.

Only two biographers have grappled at any length with this complex subject. Peter Hoffman Cruse wrote his short "Biographical Sketch of William Wirt" in 1832. It was printed in the 10th edition of *The Letters of The British Spy*. William Pendleton Kennedy, who studied law under Wirt, and emulated his mentor's many literary pursuits, wrote a ponderous, two volume, *Memoirs of the Life of William Wirt, Attorney General of the United States*, in 1849. Both biographies are difficult to obtain and unpalatable to today's modern reader.

Several modern scholars have studied and written about various portions of Wirt's life, including Dr. Joseph C. Robert, Dr. Michael Oberg, Dr. Richard Beale Davis and Dr. Joseph C. Burke, to all of whom this author is indebted. Their works are too narrow in scope to portray Wirt's life in its entirety and not readily available to most readers. But they all inspired me to take on the task of reintroducing Americans to William Wirt, an intriguing and charismatic historic figure whose thoughts, expressed through refreshingly candid personal letters and more formal published writings, are of nearly as much value now as they were almost two centuries ago. As a working journalist with an interest in history, I chose to tell Wirt's story, as much as possible, through his own words. Fortunately, there was a sufficient body of surviving letters and published material to make this possible. I hope the reader finds Wirt as fascinating as I did. And I hope this humble effort inspires others to look at Wirt's life in a new light.

Gregory K. Glassner
Madison, Virginia
April, 1997

Table of Contents

Chapter 1

A Life of Accomplishment

When William Wirt died in 1834, the United States Supreme Court adjourned and held an assembly at which Daniel Webster and Chief Justice John Marshall spoke in his honor. Wirt's funeral was attended by President Andrew Jackson, Vice President John C. Calhoun, ex-President John Quincy Adams, the entire cabinet, members of the bench and bar of the Supreme Court, officers of the Army and Navy, including Gen. Winfield Scott and many members of the House and Senate, including Henry Clay. The day after Wirt was buried, Adams gave a moving eulogy to his departed friend in a joint session of Congress.[1]

Wirt was once among the best-known public figures in America. He served for nearly 12 years as Attorney General – the longest anyone has held that position – and had served as prosecutor and defense attorney on some of the biggest court cases in the nation's history. He was also one of the nation's foremost literary figures and orators. Although Wirt never attended college, he was awarded an honorary degree by Princeton University. Less than a year before his death, Thomas Jefferson asked Wirt to serve as head of the law school at the newly formed University of Virginia, an honor Wirt declined. In 1832, Wirt lent his name as standard bearer of the quixotic Anti-Mason Party in a half-hearted attempt to wrest the presidency from Jackson and deliver it to Clay.

Born to an innkeeper's family in Maryland, and orphaned by the time he was eight years old, Wirt moved to Virginia in

1792 and was admitted to the bar at age 20. A young man with obvious potential, he was befriended by Jefferson, Madison and Monroe, who influenced, encouraged and prodded their young protégé on to far greater achievements than he had imagined possible. Wirt was appointed Clerk of the Virginia House of Delegates when he was 28 and became Chancellor of the Eastern District of Virginia when he was 30. He served in the Virginia House of Delegates from 1808-10. In 1816, President Madison appointed him U.S. District Attorney for Virginia. From 1817-1829, Wirt served two presidents, Monroe and John Quincy Adams, as U.S. Attorney General. He was the first Attorney General to hold cabinet rank and first to keep a permanent record of his decisions.

Wirt's fame as a trial lawyer paralleled his political career. In 1800, he was the youngest member of the defense team in the trial of political muckraker James Thomson Callender under the controversial Alien & Sedition Acts. In 1807, Wirt became the youngest member of the prosecution team in that era's Trial of the Century – the treason case against former Vice President Aaron Burr. Although Burr was acquitted, Wirt's four-hour summation of the "Blennerhassett Affair" stands as one of the notable examples of courtroom oratory. As Attorney General, Wirt was involved in such landmark decisions as *McCullough vs. Maryland*, the Dartmouth College case and the New York Steamboat case. After leaving office, he twice represented the Cherokee Tribe against the State of Georgia before the U.S. Supreme Court.

Wirt achieved early literary fame in 1803 for "The Letters of the British Spy," a controversial series of satirical essays on American society and prominent lawyers and politicians. These were followed in 1804-5 with "The Rainbow Association," a second series of 26 essays written by Wirt and others. In 1808, Wirt again took up pen and jumped to the defense of his friend James Madison. From 1810-13, he and his cohorts penned 33 "Old Bachelor" essays. In 1817, he wrote the first biography of Patrick Henry, the voice of the American Revolution. Again, it was a work widely read, praised by some, and pummeled by others. Wirt's letters, many of which survive, demonstrated a natural flair with words and a finely tuned sense of humor.

A serious student of oratory, Wirt took great pride in how his courtroom appearances were received by judge, jury and the ever-present gallery. Several of Wirt's courtroom summations live on today in legal textbooks. He was often called upon to give speeches, particularly on patriotic holidays, when his flowery style was most appropriate. When the U.S. Congress paid a joint tribute to Thomas Jefferson and John Adams after their deaths in 1826, it was Wirt who was called upon to deliver the address.[2]

Throughout his life, Wirt struggled to maintain balance between his practical and industrious German-Swiss heritage and a tendency to while away days and nights in high-spirited revelry and animated discourse on a wide variety of subjects. He also fought intense private battles between the persistent call to serve in public office and the necessity of making a living and providing his children with more financial security than he had experienced in his youth. Wirt became an avid, almost obsessive champion of a broad education for young men and women, and devoted a great deal of his time to train and advise young lawyers and to steer bright young minds toward literary and oratorical excellence. For many years after his death, "William Wirt Societies" and literary institutes flourished in a number of American cities.[3]

Yet, Wirt is known today, insofar as he is known at all, as much for what he failed to accomplish, or for the honors he declined, as for the heights he scaled. He refused a "sure seat" in Congress, when Jefferson offered it in 1808, and declined subsequent offers to run for the U.S. Senate. Wirt declined the offer to head up the law school and serve as first president of the University of Virginia. Wirt often lamented the fact that his law career did not permit him to devote more time to literary pursuits. His biography of Henry was planned to be the first of a series on the Founding Fathers of the nation. But his plans to retire comfortably to a life of letters were curtailed by his death at age 62. Today, William Wirt is chiefly remembered in the indexes of books about Patrick Henry, Aaron Burr, Thomas Jefferson, James Madison, James Monroe and John Quincy Adams, or in end notes to studies of 19th-Century literature.

Perhaps Wirt has been relegated to obscurity because historians have found him so difficult to classify. Was he best known as a lawyer, essayist, biographer, orator, or public servant? In truth, he was well known as all of these to his contemporaries.

Chapter 2:

A Difficult Youth

Many leaders in the early days of this nation were born of privilege, the recipients of a fine education and all the advantages accorded to the sons and daughters of well-to-do families. Such was not the case with William Wirt, orphaned at the tender age of eight and shunted off by relatives to one boarding school after another. Yet from this unsteady beginning would come the drive and depth of character that would guide him through a successful adulthood. Wirt recorded many of his childhood memories, perhaps envisioning an autobiography. But these abruptly cut off at age 11 and never resume. His personal observations about his life, even at that tender age, however, provide some insights into the man he would become.

Wirt was born in Bladensburg, Maryland, on November 8, 1772. His father, Jacob Wirt, was from Switzerland; his mother, Henrietta, of German birth. Jacob and his brother Jasper settled in Bladensburg, where they prospered. Jacob operated a small tavern and, by the time of William's birth, had purchased several properties in the village. William was the sixth and last child of Jacob and Henrietta.[1]

Less than two years after William's birth, Jacob Wirt died, leaving Henrietta to care for a growing family on a limited income. Jacob Wirt's will divided a modest estate among his wife and children, Jacob, Elizabeth, Catharine, Henrietta, Uriah-Jasper and William. The elder Wirt's holdings included the tavern, stables, smith shop, a billiard room, a newly completed house and a store rented for "twenty-five pounds sterling per annum" to Cunningham and Company.[2] William Wirt's mother remarried. Wirt's stepfather was Peter Carnes, an old family friend who stepped in and paid for Jacob Wirt's funeral and assisted the Wirts with running the tavern. Henrietta Wirt fell ill and died six years after Jacob, before William's eighth birthday. It is unknown how much of the family property

4

survived that period, but divided among six children, William's share could not have been more than a modest amount.[3]

At the time of Wirt's birth, Bladensburg was a small but thriving tobacco port on a tributary of the Potomac River. Among its occupants were a number of wealthy merchants engaged in trans-Atlantic trade. Given the standards of the day, it was an attractive town to grow up in. Wirt's upbringing, for at least the first eight years of his life, was, conventionally middle class. Wirt was remembered as a "lively, shrewd, pleasant-tempered and beautiful" child who could charm adults with his quick wit and gregarious mannerisms.[4] The Revolutionary War began before he was four and did not end until he was ten. Wirt's personal memories of this great chapter of American history were sketchy at best – certainly no better than the impressions of those of us who were born during World War II or the Vietnam War. In a vignette Wirt wrote for his grandchildren, he recalled the passage of Lighthorse Harry Lee and his troops through Bladensburg on their way to support General Greene in the South:

"I remember a long line of cavalry in the street, the large beautiful horses and fine-looking men in uniform, and a particular individual who was pointed out to me as a relation to my family. His hair was loose, long, black and frizzled, and flowed over his broad shoulders, sweeping down to his saddle. General Lee, who I knew well in aftertimes, has repeatedly mentioned this individual to me as an officer (a subaltern, perhaps) of great merit; which fixes the fact that the cavalry I saw was of Lee's Legion. It extended along the street until the head of the column had turned the corner at the lower, the southern extremity of the village, before the rear came into view – a spectacle well calculated to fill the imagination, and stamp itself deeply on the memory of a boy of my age."[5]

Wirt cited another Revolutionary War incident, one in which he received the only scolding he could recall his mother giving him during their eight years together. Observing the musters of militia that occurred with frequency in Bladensburg, young Wirt was impressed with the drummers and practiced their craft "on the tables and on the floors and singing the common marches of the time, with such directness and dexterity that it attracted the attention of others." One day an elderly man gave him a small pair of blue drumsticks he had made. Wirt happened across a group of soldiers drinking in a room at the local baker's, and the baker offered him one of the soldiers' drums. "I performed with such animation and success that the soldiers were astounded," Wirt recalled. "The drum head was soon covered with as many pieces of silver coin and pennies as filled both my hands. It was on occasion of my carrying these home in triumph that my honored and beloved mother gave me a rebuke against taking money presents, which fashioned my character in that particular for life."[6]

Elisha Crown was Wirt's first schoolmaster. The school was "across the square," from his childhood home. Crown was "an Englishman; a middle-sized man, stoop-shouldered, spare, rather thin-faced and of dark complexion. He wore a suit of blue cloth, coat, waistcoat and small clothes, with black horn buttons, an old-fashioned cock-and-pinch hat... a pair of silver shoe buckles." Crown's school soon moved about a mile into the country in a log home along the Bladensburg-Georgetown Road. The land belonged to Wirt's Uncle Jasper, whose oldest daughter married the schoolmaster.[7]

Another childhood memory of Wirt's was of his aunt: "She was a tall and rather large-framed woman, with a fair complexion and a round face, that must have been handsome in her youth. She was a native of Switzerland, and had a cast of character that made her worthy of the land of William Tell. A kinder being never lived. She was full of all the charities and courtesies of life, always ready to suggest excuses for the weakness and frailties of others, yet without any frailty or weakness of her own that I could discover. She was religious, a great reader of religious books and had a large, old folio German Bible, bound either in wood or hard black leather, with silver or brass clasps. Often have I seen her read that book with streaming eyes and a voice half-choked with her feelings."[8]

Among the residents of Bladensburg in his youth, Wirt remembered Robert Dick, a quiet, thoughtful man of business, residing in a beautiful mansion, "a long white house with wings, which stood on the summit of the Eastern Ridge which overlooks the town," and Mr. Sidebotham, "a stirring, busy successful merchant, rosy from good living, who, in the old fashion of Maryland, had his bowl of toddy every day – a thorough John Bull, proud, rough, absolute and kind." At the lower end of town towards Baltimore lived "old Mr. Martin, whom we called Uncle Martin – why I know not," Wirt said. When floodwaters rose into the village the boy was treated to the spectacle of Uncle Martin "wading up to his waist, during a freshet, and harpooning the sturgeon. It was a whale fishery in miniature, and not less interesting to me at that date... His second daughter was a beautiful girl whom I can just remember.

The oldest son of my Uncle Jasper was in love with her, and I have a recollection of having heard him take leave of her, when he was going to sea to seek his fortune. He was accompanied by my eldest brother. They never returned nor were ever heard from afterwards."[9]

Wirt said he derived childhood inspiration from "a dancer on the slackwire" named Templeman. "A large wire fastened at each end of the room, near the ceiling, hung in a curve, the middle of it within twelve or fifteen inches of the floor... Templeman [was] a tall man, superbly attired in a fanciful dress; of a military air, with a drum hung over his shoulder by a scarlet scarf. It was such a picture as I had never seen. Saluting the company with dignity, he placed himself upon the wire; then giving a hand to his attendant, he was drawn to one side of the room, and being let go, swung at ease – beating the drum like a professional performer. He performed all the usual exploits, balancing hoops, swords, etc. – and to crown the whole, danced what I had never seen before, a hornpipe, in superior style... My own imitative propensity came again into play, and I became a celebrated hornpipe-dancer before I was six years of age; meaning by celebrated, such celebrity as spread through about one-third of our little village." In penning this remembrance, Wirt revealed a wry sense of humor by adding, "The image of Templeman rose before me as something of another age, or another sphere when, about forty years after I had seen him swinging in such splendor on the wire, I met in Washington a well-dressed gentleman-like person, somewhat corpulent, who was made known to me as the paragon of my childish admiration, converted into a plain citizen, and an extensive dealer in city lots."[10]

In 1779, Wirt was sent to a classical academy run by a Mr. Rogers in Georgetown, eight miles from Bladensburg. He lived at a boarding house run by a family of Quakers named Schoolfield (or Scholfield). "Friend Schoolfield was a well-set, squarebuilt, honest-faced and honest-hearted Quaker – his wife one of the best of creation," Wirt noted. Mrs. Schoolfield consoled the homesick youth. "After quieting me in some measure by her caresses, she took down her Bible and read to me the story of Joseph and his Brethren... she made me comprehend it; and in the distresses of Joseph and his father I forgot my own." Wirt confessed that he remembered far less about his year at Mr. Rogers' school, although he did remark that one of his classmates there, Richard Brent, later distinguished himself in the U.S. House of Representatives.[11]

After his mother's death, Wirt was enrolled in a classical school in Charles County, Maryland, about forty miles from Bladensburg. "This school was kept by one Hatch Dent, in the vestry house of Newport Church," Wirt remembered years later. "I was boarded by a widow lady by the name of Love, and my residence in her family forms one of the few sunny spots in the retrospect of my childhood. Mrs. Love was a small, thin old lady, a good deal bent by age, yet brisk and active. The family was composed of her and three maiden daughters, of whom the eldest, I suppose, was verging on forty and the youngest, perhaps twenty-eight."[12] The precocious child amused the Love sisters with his drumming and pipe dancing. "Besides my singing, I danced to the astonishment of the natives, and, altogether, had the reputation of a genius. Thus admired, flattered and feasted with milk and cream, *Roslin Castle* and *Clarissa Harlow*, etc., what more could a child of my age want to make him happy... I lived there, I think, as perfectly happy as a child could be who was separated from his mother and the other natural objects of his affections."[13]

Wirt's teacher in Charles County, Mr. Dent, was "a most excellent man, a sincere and pious Christian, and, I presume, a good teacher – for I was too young to judge, and, in fact, much too young for a Latin school. In the two years Johnson Carnes and myself got as far advanced as Caesar's Commentaries – though we could not have been well grounded, for when I changed to another school, I was put back to Cornelius Nepos."[14]

In 1783, Wirt was transferred to a school run by the Rev. James Hunt, a Presbyterian minister in Montgomery County. The boy was boarded at the home of Major Samuel Wade Magruder, a planter, who lived about two miles from Mr. Hunt's. "The Major showed marks of Highland extraction. He was large, robust and somewhat corpulent, with a round florid face, short curling, sandy hair, and blue-gray eyes. He was strong of limb, fiery in temperament, hospitable, warm-hearted and rough. He was a magistrate and *ex-officio,* a conservator of the peace, which, however, he was as ready on provocation, to break as to preserve. At times he was kind and playful with the boys; but woe betide the unfortunate boy or man who became the object of his displeasure!" The Major's voice, Wirt said, "I remember as the loud north wind that used to rock the house and sweep the snow-covered field. They had a large family – seven sons and four daughters."[15]

Wirt observed that "Magruder's household embraced not less than twenty white persons. To these there was a constant addition, by visitors to the young people of the family. It was, in fact, an active, bustling, merry, noisy family, always in motion, and often in commotion. To me it was painfully contrasted with the small, quiet, affectionate establishment of Mrs. Love. There I had been the petted child and supreme object of attention. Here I was lost in the multitude, unnoticed, unthought of, and left to make my way and take care of myself as well as I could... I had been spoiled by indulgence, and was really unfit to take care of myself. I did not know how to go about it... Young as I was, I had reflection enough to compare the two scenes in which I had lived, to feel my present desolation, and to sigh over the past. The tune of *Roslin Castle* never recurred to my memory without filling my eyes with tears. I was a small, feebly-grown, delicate boy; an orphan, and a poor one too: but these circumstances seemed rather to invite than to allay the hostility of this fierce young man," Wirt said, noting that he often went to bed early to be by himself, his thoughts and his daydreams of ambition. "I looked forward to the time when I should be a young man and should have my own office of two rooms, my own servant and the means of receiving and entertaining my friends with elegant liberality, my horse and fine equipment, a rich wardrobe, and these all recommended by such manners and accomplishments as should again restore me to such favor and affectionate intercourse as I had known at Mrs. Love's."[16]

The following ten years of his life are sketchier in nature, leaving earlier biographers without detailed memoirs or the prodigious correspondence Wirt generated in his later years. Young Wirt remained at Hunt's school in Montgomery County until 1787, living with the schoolmaster's family the final two years. There he took advantage of a good library including two globes and some instruments for scientific demonstrations. He studied "the old dramas," *Josephus, Guy of Warwick, Peregrine Pickle,* the writings of Pope and Addison and Horne's *Elements of Criticism*, as well as the basics of astronomy and physics. According to 19th century biographer John Pendleton Kennedy, Wirt, later in life, lamented "the habit of immothodical reading which, acquired in early youth, had, as he supposed, somewhat injuriously diverted his time from systematic study." Hunt encouraged his pupil's tentative forays into poetry and prose. Reading that Pope first composed verse at age 12, Wirt, then 13, attempted to emulate that feat. Although

Wirt was disappointed in the results, Dent encouraged him to take up pen again.[17]

When Hunt's school closed in 1787, Wirt was 15 years old and he had exhausted his share of his family's money. Fortunately for him, there was no shortage of benefactors willing to help a bright young man who did his best to be engaging to both schoolmates and adults. The first of these was Peter Carnes, the Maryland lawyer and tobacco planter in Charles County, whose professional endeavors first brought him to Bladensburg and the public house kept by Jacob Wirt. After marrying the widow Wirt, Carnes financed the education of Elizabeth Wirt, William's older sister, and contributed to the upkeep of her youngest brother. After Henrietta's death, Carnes managed the Wirt family affairs for several years. In 1783, however, Carnes handed those responsibilities off to Jacob Wirt's unpredictable brother, Jasper, and began a brief flirtation with lighter-than-air vehicles. Carnes made what is believed to be the first passenger balloon flight in America on June 23, 1784. His next attempt, however, was branded a disastrous failure. Carnes then moved to Albany, Georgia, taking several nephews, and Wirt's sister Elizabeth with him. There he married Elizabeth, becoming both stepfather and brother-in-law to William Wirt. Although not as shocking as this might seem today, Wirt never mentioned that Carnes had been married to his mother.[18]

Another benefactor was Benjamin Edwards, whose son Ninian was Wirt's friend and classmate when Hunt's school disbanded. Ninian had given his father a copy of the constitution of their moot court. A former member of the Maryland Legislature, Edwards was sufficiently impressed with the thinking that went into that document that he invited Wirt to join their household at Mount Pleasant as a private tutor to Ninian and his two cousins. Edwards was well-versed in literature as well as law and put another fine library at Wirt's disposal. Wirt was grateful for this opportunity. After he achieved success, he wrote Edwards, saying, "You have taught me to love you like a parent. Well, indeed may I do so, since to you, to the influence of your conversation, your precepts and your example in the most critical and decisive period of my life, I owe whatever of useful or good there may be in the bias of my mind and character. Continue then, I implore you, to think of me as a son, and teach your children to regard me as a brother." (The relationship of tutor to family, which lasted for 20 months, benefited both parties. Ninian, Wirt's former classmate and pupil, achieved success of his own, serving as the first Territorial Governor of Illinois, and later Senator and Governor after statehood.) Edwards sensed that his son's young tutor was destined for a career in law, and he made an effort to steer him in his studies, counsel him on the art of oratory and provide him with role models. Pointing to Dorsey and Pinkney, two up-and-coming attorneys in the area, he told Wirt, "Dorsey, whom you so much admire, and Pinkney whom you will admire still more when you shall have seen him, are making their own way to distinction under as great disadvantages as any you have to encounter."[19]

Although productive, Wirt's stay with the Edwards family was cut short when he became ill, showing symptoms of consumption. On the advice of physician and friends, the 17-year-old went by horseback to Georgia to spend the winter of 1789. There he stayed with his sister Elizabeth and her new husband. Although Wirt left no record of his adventures it was a daunting journey for a sickly teenager. Despite the hardship of the journey, the Georgia winter seemed to agree with him. He recovered from his "pulmonary complaint" and returned to Maryland in the spring. Wirt wrote later that had it not been for this escape from the Maryland winter and the fervent sermons of the neighborhood Baptist minister, he would have "died in a lunatic asylum" or "become a preacher."[20]

At 17, Wirt was poised for adulthood. He settled at Montgomery Court House for a year and entered into the study of law under William P. Hunt, the son of his old schoolmaster. Wirt was urged to look to Virginia as a fertile field in which a young lawyer-to-be could complete his training and hone his skills. "While with Mr. Hunt," Wirt wrote Carnes, "a friend informed me of a very advantageous station for a lawyer in the State of Virginia. Everybody urged me to seize it. The law in Virginia required from me twelve months' residence in the state, and a previous examination by three of the Judges of the General Court. I removed my residence immediately to Virginia."[21] As it would transpire, it would prove a fortuitous decision. The orphan would find a career, a home, and a host of prominent new benefactors in the Old Dominion.

Chapter 3

Established in Virginia

Wirt moved to Fredericksburg, Virginia, and continued his studies in the law under Thomas Swann, an acquaintance and former schoolmate of Tom Carnes. Swann was a member of the bar in Virginia and in Washington, and had served as District Attorney of the United States in Washington. Having disposed of his remaining claim to family property in Maryland, Wirt established legal residence in Virginia. After only five months under Swann's tutelage, Wirt applied for a license to practice law. He was examined by a panel of three judges and deemed fit. In his letter to Peter Carnes, Wirt alluded to "a manoeuvre" that removed the objection of non-residence."[1]

After but seventeen months of training under practicing attorneys, and armed with a "legal library" that by his own admission consisted of one copy of *Blackstone*, two volumes of *Don Quixote* and one volume of *Tristram Shandy*, he set off for Culpeper Courthouse in the autumn of 1792 to begin his practice of law. In addition to a minimal legal education, no experience, and the handicap of practicing law in an unfamiliar part of the country, Wirt had one more disadvantage – no client. The problem of a client was soon rectified when Wirt met at the courthouse another young lawyer who had yet to get his feet wet, one who happened to have a client. The two novices quickly agreed to a joint debut. Their case concerned assault and battery with a joint judgment against three men, two of whom had been released following the judgment. The third, their client, had been imprisoned, but felt entitled to the same treatment as his cohorts. Wirt and his equally inexperienced co-counsel presented their case in the form of a motion. In those days, the bench consisted of ordinary justices of the peace, with elder members of the bar frequently interposing as *amici curiae*, or informers of the court's conscience. Wirt's new-found friend opened the argument but quickly found himself up against these advisors to the court, who denied that a release of one miscreant after

12

judgment automatically allowed the release of the other. The senior lawyers also found fault with the form of the proceeding. This reception so angered Wirt that he flew to his co-counsel's defense, driving home their point with alacrity and conviction. Impressed by the 20-year-old's spunk, a senior lawyer, General John Minor of Fredericksburg, stepped in as an auxiliary, remarking that he also was *amicus curiae*, and, "perhaps, as much entitled to act as such as others; in which capacity he would state his conviction of the propriety of the motion and that the court was not at liberty to disregard it." Bolstered by this support, the two young lawyers prevailed, winning their first case.[2]

Wirt was grateful for Miner's assistance. "There was never a more finished and engaging gentleman, nor one of a more warm, honest and affectionate heart," he wrote years later. "He was as brave a man and as true a patriot as ever lived. He was a most excellent lawyer too, with a most persuasive flow of eloquence, simple, natural and graceful, and most affecting wherever there was room for pathos; and his pathos was not artificial rhetoric; it was of that true sort which flows from a feeling heart and noble mind. He was my firm and constant friend from that day through a long life; and took occasion, several times in after years, to remind me of his prophecy, and to insist on my obligation to sustain his 'prophetic reputation.'"[3]

Despite this initial success, it can be presumed that the 20-year-old lawyer was not immediately showered with riches nor besieged by clients clamoring for representation. Wirt supplemented his income and accessed the gracious living for which he had already developed a taste by signing on as a tutor for the family of Henry Fry. A recovering alcoholic who embraced Methodism in 1774, Fry lived at *Elim* (Hebrew for Seven Springs, Seven Palms and Peace), at the junction of the Robinson River and Meander Run, now known as Crooked Run. Fry had been the tax collector of Buckingham County when he took a doctor's advice to cure a fever with liquor and "soon found the remedy to be worse than the disease." He moved his family to Culpeper County "in shame" in 1766 and built a plantation on 1,000 acres of land he had inherited from his father. Located between the towns of Culpeper and Orange, Elim became part of the new Madison County, when it was formed by an act of the General Assembly in late 1792. Fry found religion and his home became a regular preaching place for Methodist ministers for the next 40 years. Fry was appointed General Steward of the sixth annual Conference of the Methodist Church in Leesburg in

1778. Although he owned slaves, Fry was a mover for the General Emancipation Bill when he represented Madison County in the General Assembly from 1785-86. (Fry's father was Col. Joshua Fry, one of the first Englishmen to patent land in the area. The senior Fry taught mathematics at the College of William & Mary from 1728 to 1732 and was a member of the House of Burgesses. He served as Justice of the Peace in Albemarle County from 1745-48. and was George Washington's senior in command of Virginia Forces in 1754. Col. Fry owned 4,000 acres of land in Virginia, including the 1,000 acres on which his son built Elim. Col. Fry also worked as a surveyor with Peter Jefferson, father of Thomas Jefferson. The original Fry-Jefferson Map of Virginia is on display at Harvard.)[4]

As tutor to such a prominent family, Wirt increased his client base and gained entry to the intellectual circles of Culpeper, Orange and Albemarle counties. The Frys were close friends to the Jeffersons and the Madisons. The Madisons ran a mill on the Rapidan River just a few miles from Elim. Montpelier and Monticello were less than a day's ride away. Wirt set up a law office in a small building located in a field near Elim and whiled away the lapses between clients and court appearances by fishing in the Robinson River, writing amusing ditties and being an amiable companion to Fry's 13 children. Henry Fry frequently preached in neighboring Orange County. It was there, accompanied by Fry's son Wesley, that Wirt first heard James Waddell, the "Blind Preacher," whom he later immortalized in one of his "British Spy" essays.[5] Life as an adjunct member of the Fry family was not without friction, however. In his diary, Orange County's Col. Francis Taylor mentioned that Fry dismissed Wirt after one year because of his supposed "infidel views." Wirt healed this rift, however, writing several letters to Fry denying the charge. Wirt was rehired for a second year. As an ex-alcoholic, Fry may also have had other concerns about the fitness of the tutor he hired for his children. In a notation in Taylor's diary, Andrew Glassell Grinnan stated, "this Wirt practiced law in Orange, Madison Culpeper & Albemarle whilst at Mr. Frys (sic). He drank & was often drunken." Grinnan also noted that Wirt's law office was in a small building near the "old Clifton house where Dr. & Mrs [Teke] live [ed] in 1892."[6]

Culpeper County was surveyed by George Washington in 1749. The Town was established in 1759. When Wirt arrived in the county, it already had thousands of residents and was on the verge of being subdivided into two counties, creating additional legal business. Residents of the lower third of the county petitioned for a new county in 1791. The act to create Madison County, named for Congressman James Madison and his family, was approved in December, 1792. The first court day was held in April, 1793. On the second Court Day of Madison County, held in June, 1793, Wirt was certified to practice law in the newly formed county.[7] Although known later for his eloquence, Wirt, at 20, had only vestigial skills along these lines. Cruse noted that "His utterance was still faulty. A friend who knew him a little after this period says, that when heated by argument, his ideas seemed to outstrip his power of expression; his tongue appeared too large; he clipped some of his words sadly; his voice, sweet and musical in conversation grew loud and harsh, his articulation rapid, indistinct and imperfect."[8] But there was time and opportunity for Wirt to hone his skills, increase his knowledge of the law, and practice his delivery. The Virginia courts of the time were true circuits, with the lawyers traveling from county to county on horseback to ply their trade on court days, develop a broader clientele and further sharpen their skills.

Within a few years, Wirt had expanded his practice from Culpeper and Madison counties to the neighboring counties of Albemarle, Orange, Louisa and Fluvanna. By 1794, the young lawyer had ventured as far south as Henry County on the North Carolina border in search of legal business. His friends described him in those days as a happy and carefree companion who relished the forensic opportunities of the courtroom and the social activities of court days more than the technical aspects of law. "It may be true," one biographer observed, "that his studies were not so conversant with the deeps of legal science, as one might demand from the ambitious lawyer, and even that he doffed aside the sometimes admonishing hopes of a solid professional fame; but it can scarcely be true that an active and apprehensive mind, such as his was, was suffered either to rest for want of use, or to devote itself to frivolous or useless subjects."[9]

In 1795, Wirt landed his first big criminal case, the defense of two white men, Marshall and Patterson, who were accused of homicide by whipping a slave to death. In his argument, Wirt said he could not justify slavery, "that foul disgrace to men who affect to glory in the hallowed name of liberty." But, Wirt added, slavery was "the guilt of the nation," and not solely that of the defendants. The slave's death did not occur from cruel and unusual punishment – cruel perhaps, but far from unusual in that day. "And is not a cowhide an usual instrument of correction?" Wirt asked.[10]

Away from the courtroom, Wirt quickly gained a reputation as a bon vivant who savored the brotherhood of the bar and the camaraderie of evenings spent in rural taverns and gracious manors every bit as much, if not more so, than the heated courtroom battles he fought during the day. Though a stranger when he arrived, the former orphan was embraced and adopted by the leading lights of local society and became an amiable companion for their sons and nephews as they rode the circuit together. The handsome and outgoing young man from Maryland became "an admired object in the court house during the day, a leading spirit in the evening coterie; eloquent on the field of justice, sustaining his client's cause with a shrewd and sometimes brilliant skill; not less eloquent at the table or mess-room, where his faculties were allowed to expatiate through another range, and where he gave reins to the wit and mirth which shook the root-tree."[11]

These travels brought Wirt in contact with the family of Dr. George Gilmer, who lived at Pen Park near Charlottesville. Gilmer was from a Scottish family that came to Virginia in the early days of the colony. He journeyed abroad to study medicine in Edinburgh and enjoyed a large practice. Gilmer served in the Colonial House of Burgesses and has been called the "Sam Adams of Albemarle" for his patriotic zeal and enthusiasm for the Revolution. He was a leading member of the 1774 Citizens Committee and was a lieutenant of the Albemarle Volunteers, persuading his militia unit to march on Williamsburg in a show of force against Lord Dunmore in the spring of 1775. He fought with distinction in the Revolutionary War, participated in the state Constitution Committee, and helped draft the Virginia Declaration of Rights. Dr. Gilmer was Sheriff of Albemarle County in 1787 and also served in the House of Delegates. He was a close personal friend and political ally of Jefferson, Monroe and Madison. Pen Park was located just across the river from Monticello, and Gilmer also served as Jefferson's physician.[12]

It is not clear if Dr. Gilmer gazed across the dinner table at young Wirt and sought him as a son-in-law, or if Wirt and Mildred, Gilmer's oldest child, exchanged coy glances and took it from there. A friend described Wirt, in his mid-20s, as "highly engaging and prepossessing. His figure was strikingly elegant and commanding, with a face of the first order of masculine beauty, animated and expressing high intellect. His manners took the tone of his heart: they were frank, open and cordial, and his conversation, to which his reading and early pursuits had given a classic tinge, was very polished, gay and witty. Altogether, he was a most fascinating companion, and to those of his own age, irresistibly and universally winning." Short and graceless, Mildred was not a ravishing beauty. But she was "kind, cheerful, intellectual, noted for her good sense and just observation." And she was well-connected – just the combination a poor but ambitious young lawyer might seek in a wife. On May 28, 1795, Wirt and Mildred Gilmer were married in a gala ceremony at Pen Park. Wirt moved into the good doctor's spacious home, shared in the elegant hospitality it offered, and availed himself of the large library, which included the works of Hooker, Boyle, Locke, Barrow, South, Bacon and Milton. Although he was 14 to 29 years their junior, Wirt became closely acquainted with Monroe, Madison and Jefferson, who had already embarked on political paths that would take them to the highest office in the young nation. They found in Wirt a willing listener and an ardent supporter of their political views. In return, they encouraged and prodded their young protégé to parlay his legal and rhetorical skills into a more public life than he envisioned or desired.[13]

Chapter 4

Useful Alliances Forged

The five years Wirt spent at Pen Park were happy times, for the most part, and a period during which his professional and social prospects grew by leaps and bounds. As Kennedy observed, "Pen Park exhibited just such a combination of rare and pleasant appurtenances as are likely to make the best impressions upon the mind of an ingenious and ambitious youth, and to inspire him with zeal in the cultivation of virtue and knowledge." Dr. Gilmer was a frequent visitor to Monticello. His fourth son Francis, who came to know Wirt more as an older brother than brother-in-law, was educated under Thomas Jefferson's direction and later studied the law under Wirt. Jefferson also undoubtedly saw in Wirt fresh clay in need of molding.

The Gilmer family, to which Wirt remained close throughout his life, is also known for Dr. Gilmer's grandson, Thomas Walker Gilmer, (1802-1844), son of Dr. George Gilmer III, a lawyer and newspaper editor who served as Governor and Congressman from Virginia, and Secretary of the Navy under Pres. Tyler until his tragic death in the explosion of the mammoth gun "Peacemaker," aboard the USS Princeton on Feb. 28, 1844. Much contemporary insight into Wirt's character can be gleaned from his correspondence with Francis Gilmer and a biographical sketch written by him in 1816 and published in 1828 in a collection, *Sketches, Essays and Translations*. Dr. Gilmer died two years after the marriage of his daughter to Wirt. Wirt was named an executor, and a portion of Gilmer's estate, was left to the couple in Dr. Gilmer's will. Wirt built a house at Rose Hill, adjacent to Pen Park, but because the Wirts had no children, they spent much of their time in the Gilmer mansion. For at least one season, Wirt supervised the upbringing of Dr. Gilmer's children, until Jefferson assumed that responsibility. Most of Wirt's correspondence from this period is dated "Pen Park," indicating that he still regarded Dr.

Gilmer's house as his principal residence and that the Wirts had a hand in running the household after Dr. Gilmer's death.[1]

A friend from the Pen Park years described Wirt, as he knew him then: "His figure was strikingly elegant and commanding, with a face of the first order of masculine beauty, animated, and expressing high intellect. His manners took the tone of his heart; they were frank; open and cordial; and his conversation, to which his reading and early pursuits had given a classic tinge, was very polished, gay and witty."[2] One letter, dated 1799, is a reply to a dinner invitation from Wirt's friend and fellow lawyer, Dabney Carr of Dunlora (Jefferson's nephew). It provides some insight into Wirt's confident, but lighthearted and whimsical nature during this period:

I cannot go over to see you to-day, my good friend. And I have almost as many, and as solid reasons for my conduct, as Doctor Ross had for not wearing stockings with boots. The first of his was, that he had no stockings, and his catechiser was satisfied. Let us see if you will be as candid.

Firstly — We have a troop of visiting cousins here, who have come from afar, and whom we cannot, you know, decently invite to leave our house.

Secondly — We have, perhaps, finer lamb and lettuce to-day, for dinner, than have ever graced the table of Epicurus, not meaning to imply any thing to the dishonor of Donlora or Dunlora, or something, I forget what.

Thirdly — Mr. Ormsby is here, who brings an historical, topographical, critical, chronological and fantastical account of Kentucky and its inhabitants.

Fourthly — To conclude, we have determined that, immediately upon the receipt of this, you are to start for this place; for, you observe, that the same reasons which justify my staying at home, prove the propriety, and, I hope you will think, necessity of your coming hither.[3]

Dabney Carr was the youngest son of Dabney Carr Sr., who was married to Thomas Jefferson's sister and served in the House of Burgesses before its disbandment, speaking eloquently for the formation of a Continental Congress. The elder Carr died in May, 1773, a month after his youngest son was born. Jefferson took an active role in the education of his three nephews, Peter, who favored the rural life and philosophical study; Samuel (later Col. Samuel Carr), who followed the political path, representing his district in the state Senate; and Dabney, who practiced law and became a distinguished judge.

Another young lawyer friend of Wirt's was James Barbour of Orange County (1775-1842), who served in the House of Delegates from 1796-1812, was Governor of Virginia from 1812-1814, and U.S. Senator from 1815-1825. (Close friends as young attorneys, Barbour and Wirt would be reunited in the cabinet of Pres. John Quincy Adams from 1825 to 1828, Barbour as Secretary of War, Wirt as Attorney General.) Barbour was a resolute defender of state's rights, but held the institution of slavery in low regard. His younger brother Philip was Speaker of the House of Representatives from 1821-23 and Associate Justice of the U.S. Supreme Court from 1837 until his death in 1841. (John Strode Barbour Sr. (1790-1855), cousin of James and Philip, also represented their district in Congress.)

With such friends as these, in addition to benefactors Jefferson, Madison and Monroe, there is little wonder that Wirt would periodically be persuaded to venture into the arena of politics and public service, despite his protestations that he needed to tend to the more lucrative business of law and could not afford the dalliances in the limelight that eroded the fortunes of many of the political leaders of the day. Throughout his life, Wirt staunchly maintained that his nose was in constant contact with the grindstone. But there is evidence that he was often the life of the party while en route to the courtroom or in discussing the day's events far into the evening. At least one incident related by Kennedy bears this out:

James Barbour, Dabney Carr and Wirt were on their customary journey to neighboring Fluvanna county to attend court in "the State of Flu," as they jokingly referred to it. "They had been amusing each other with the usual prankishness which characterized their intercourse. Wirt was noted for making clever speeches, as they rode together... Sometimes he rode ahead of his companions, and, waiting for them by the road side, welcomed them, in an oration of mock gravity, to the confines of 'the State of Flu,' representing himself to be one of its dignitaries, sent there to receive the distinguished persons into whom he had transformed the young attorneys of the circuit. These exhibitions, and others of the same kind, are said to have been of the most comic spirit, and to have afforded many a laugh to the actors."[4]

In another incident, the three friends stopped to dine and spend the night at Carr's Brook in Albemarle County, the residence of Peter Carr. There Barbour entertained everyone with a discourse on his merits as well as those of his two friends. "You, Dabney, have indulged a vision of judicial eminence. You shall be gratified, and shall hold a seat on the Bench of the Court of Appeals of Virginia," Barbour said. "Your fortune, William, shall conduct you to the Attorney Generalship of the United States, where you shall have harder work to do than making bombastic speeches in the woods of Albemarle. As for myself, I shall be content to take my seat in the Senate of the United States."[5] While quite possibly apocryphal, considering the accuracy of the predictions, this story sheds light on the interplay between these three talented and ambitious young men. (Wirt, Barbour and Carr wrote prodigiously in later life, but were apparently too busy learning the law and living life to the fullest to have written much about themselves in their early years.)

Some law was practiced, despite the lawyerly shenanigans and social whirl in which Wirt found himself during those years. Jefferson threw him some work, and Wirt also acted as an agent for the federal government in the case of *U.S. v. Samuel Munday*. Munday was charged with operating illegally as an auctioneer, having failed to pay the tax and licensing fees pushed through by Alexander Hamilton as Washington's Secretary of the Treasury. The jury found Munday guilty, but the verdict was later set aside on a technicality.[6] Col. Taylor of Orange continued to employ Wirt as well. In his diary entry for March 27, 1798, Taylor talks about hiring Wirt to handle the defense in "the suits brought against me by McCall & c." On May 29, Taylor mentioned paying Wirt "4 dollars for fees, & advice in the Pet'n & Summons, McCall Smellie & Co. and Capias George McCall & Co. against Taylors Exors."[7]

There are some indications that Wirt's zest for life and desire to party well into the night exceeded even the somewhat liberal standards for young gentlemen in the 1790s. Kennedy beats around the bush on these topics in his biography: "I do not wish to conceal the fact that at this time of the life of Mr. Wirt, he was not altogether free from the censure of having sometime yielded to the spells of the tempter and fallen into some occasional irregularities of conduct. I am aware that this charge has been made in graver form, with some amplitude of detail and circumstance.... An unbounded hospitality amongst the gentlemen of the country, opened every door to the indulgence of convivial habits... Every dinner party was a revel; every ordinary visit was a temptation. The gentlemen of the bar, especially, indulged in a license of free living, which habitually approached the confines of excess, and often overstepped them." Lawyers in those days (and to a limited extent now) gathered under one roof after court "to rehearse their pleasant adventures, and to act flowing the currents of mirth and good humor – 'to make a night of it,' as the phrase is, kept merry by the stimulants of good cheer," Kennedy added. Wirt, he said, was "an admired object in the court house during the day, a leading spirit in the evening coterie; eloquent on the field of justice, sustaining his client's cause with a shrewd and sometimes brilliant skill; not less eloquent at the table or the mess-room, where his faculties were allowed to expatiate through another range, and where he gave reins to the wit and mirth which shook the roof-tree. We may not wonder that, in the symposia of these days, the graver maxims of caution were forgotten, and that the enemy of human happiness, always lying at lurch to make prey of the young, should sometimes steal upon his guard and make his virtue prisoner... The too frequent recurrence of these misadventures in that day, have furnished food for much gross calumny in regard to him, and have led to the fabrication of coarse and disgusting charges of vulgar excess, which I am persuaded are utterly groundless."[8] While Kennedy overdid his defense of Wirt, the vague references to demon rum and "excesses" leaves us wondering whether Wirt, at this time of his life, was merely a heavy social imbiber or a drunken sot. One must also take into account the fact that, though Wirt was not as heavily immersed in politics as his benefactors, he was prominent enough to make enemies. Mudslinging is not a new concept and certainly flourished in the early days of this nation.

It is clear, however, that Wirt relished the social scene he entered through his wife's family and his new professional connections. Although many of the acquaintances he made there continued to be fast friends for life, the Pen Park phase of his life came crashing to a halt with the death of Mildred Gilmer Wirt on Sept. 17, 1799. The inscription Wirt had carved on her tombstone, which was very likely written by him, concisely sums up his great affection for his first wife:

Come round her tomb each object of desire,
Each purer frame inflamed with purer fire,
Be all that's good, that cheers and softens life,
The tender sister, daughter, friend and wife,
And when your virtues you have counted o'er,
Then view this marble and be vain no more[9]

Chapter 5

A Change of Venue

Although he was no stranger to death, having lost his mother and father at a tender age and, as a child watching soldiers march off to Revolutionary War battles, Wirt was shaken considerably by the death of his wife, Mildred, just five years after they were married and three years after her father died. The young lawyer's new-found friends and advisors were sufficiently concerned that they urged him to explore new endeavors. They persuaded him to become a candidate for Clerk of the House of Delegates and backed up his candidacy with the political support to secure him the position.

Wirt's friend and fellow lawyer, James Barbour, had been elected to the House of Delegates in 1796 and would serve there for 14 years, the last three as Speaker. James Madison was in the middle of a two-year stint as a delegate, following eight years in Congress. (In 1799 he wrote the Virginia Resolutions in protest against the 1798 federal Alien and Sedition Acts.) James Monroe was in his first year as Virginia's Governor. Although he held no office at the time, Thomas Jefferson was preparing for a second bid for the Presidency, having lost to John Adams in his first attempt in 1796. Jefferson was not without influence, of course, and he could share Wirt's pain, having lost his wife after only ten years of marriage. The pathway to the clerk's job was paved by virtue of the Republicans regaining control of the Legislature. John Stewart, the incumbent clerk, was identified with the Federalists. The position occupied only a few of the winter months, allowing the person holding it to pursue other interests the remainder of the year. Wirt won the job by a vote of 90-49. For a 27-year-old lawyer who had resided in Virginia only eight years, the clerk's post, which paid $145 per week for six to eight weeks of work each year, was a high honor. Wirt's predecessors included such luminaries as George Wythe and Edmund Randolph. Wirt obtained lodgings with Meriwether Jones, editor of the Republican newspaper, the *Examiner,* and later became the roommate of George Hay, Monroe's son-in-law.[1]

The session of 1800 was expected to be a lively one. The Resolutions of 1798 were still fresh in the minds of everyone, and questions about the Constitution and state's rights were hot topics. Patrick Henry, the old revolutionary turned staunch Federalist, came out of retirement and won election to the House of Delegates. As a result, the fur was expected to fly. But Henry died before talking his seat, and Wirt, already gaining a reputation as a man of words, would never hear this legend speak. The coincidence of this may have prompted Wirt, some years hence, to tackle Henry as a fit subject for what he envisioned as the first of a series of biographies on the Founding Fathers. As Clerk of the House, Wirt fell heir to many stories about Henry. He also met a whole host of new political leaders, including William Branch Giles of Amelia, John Taylor of Caroline and Wilson Cary Nicholas, all anti-federalist allies of Madison and Barbour. Wirt would be reaffirmed as clerk in two more elections, serving in that post until February 1802.[2]

Wirt's law practice received a much needed boost in the spring of 1800, when he was invited to be the youngest member of the defense team engaged by political scandal-monger James Thomson Callender, one of the first to be prosecuted under the new Alien and Sedition Laws. Callender's sole redeeming quality, it seems, was a willingness to attack whomever sought or held the presidency, regardless of party affiliation. He was an equal-opportunity slanderer, who would have felt at home, 200 years later, working for a supermarket tabloid or political action committee. Washington, Adams and Jefferson all chafed under Callender's blistering attacks, although Jefferson originally thought of Callender as a useful ally against the Federalists. Samuel Chase, the presiding federal judge over the Richmond Circuit, brought charges against Callender for a pamphlet called, "The Prospect before us," which attacked the Adams administration. Two respected Richmond lawyers, George Hay and Phillip Norborne Nicholas, were selected as counsel for Callender. Wirt, who had been practicing law less than eight years, was named an associate, at Jefferson's request.[3]

Callender was convicted. The case against him was clear-cut under the existing statutes. The case received more notoriety than it perhaps deserved because of the controversial nature of the law Callender was accused of violating and the conduct of Justice Chase and the defense team. A crusty and imperious judge, Chase delighted in browbeating defense attorneys, and this quirk was no more apparent than during Callender's short trial. The only defense put up by Wirt and his more seasoned associates was that the law under which Callender was being tried was unconstitutional and that the jury had a right to rule on this question. Chase had none of that and repeatedly interrupted Wirt and his associates, mocking them with rude gestures. Fed up, the three defense attorneys stalked out of the court, abandoning the defense in a memorable example of judicial theatrics. "So the three young lawyers trooped out of court, with their papers bundled up. Hay led the van, and young Wirt, with his laughing eye and sly waggish face, casting queer glances, no doubt, right and left amongst the bar inside of the railing and the spectators outside, brought up the rear," Kennedy observed.[4]

When Jefferson became President in 1801, he pardoned all who had been convicted under the sedition laws, including Callender. This did not satisfy the vituperative Scotsman, however. When Jefferson failed to reward him with the position of Postmaster of Richmond, Callender hired out to the Federalists and turned his poison pen on his former benefactor. It was Callender who first printed the rumors of Jefferson's mulatto children by slave Sally Hemings. Callender's stories in the Richmond *Recorder* referring to Jefferson's "Congo harem... black Venus" and "Dusky Sally" were picked up by Federalist newspapers throughout the nation. That sad chapter of American journalism ended in July, 1803, when Callender's body was found in three feet of water in the James River. The official verdict was that he had been drinking heavily, as was his habit, and drowned accidentally. Historian Virginius Dabney noted it was possible Callender's death was no accident.[5]

The Callender trial would pop up again in 1804 when impeachment proceedings against Chase were brought before Congress a year after Callender's death. Chase's conduct in the Callender trial, another trial involving the Alien and Sedition laws and a subsequent speech to a Maryland grand jury were the basis of the accusations against him. Although Jefferson was President and the tide had turned somewhat against the Federalists, Congress did not buy the charges against Chase. The Senate acquitted him on March 5, 1805, and he remained on the bench until his death in 1811. Wirt was not called upon to testify against Chase. Cruse reported that Chase later remarked to a mutual friend, "They did not summon him on my trial; had I known it, I might have summoned him myself; yet it was only to that young man that I said anything exceptionable, or which I have thought of with regret since."[6]

In a testament to his standing in Richmond, Wirt was selected by the Democratic-Republican party to deliver the speech commemorating the anniversary of the Declaration of Independence on July 4, 1800. Although not one of Wirt's more notable oratorical outings, it sufficed. He would be called to the rostrum on a variety of ceremonial occasions from this point on. Richmond in this day, Kennedy observed, was noted for "its choice spirits, its men of wit and pleasure, and its manifold inducements to tax the discretion of those who had no great store of that commodity."[7] Wirt's legislative post and the challenge of establishing a law practice in the state capital helped him overcome his grief over the loss of his wife. And if that didn't work, there was ample opportunity to drown his sorrows in the wine, whiskey and brandy dispensed with abandon at the social functions that have always accompanied the political process.

A very eligible widower, Wirt also had the opportunity to meet as fine a selection of marriage prospects as Richmond had to offer during his three-year sojourn there. The one he chose was Elizabeth Gamble, the 17-year-old daughter of Col. Robert Gamble, a wealthy Richmond merchant. Col. Gamble was known to practice a very liberal hospitality. His table and fireside were familiar to many, and it was in one of these settings that the new Clerk of the House met his future second wife. Kennedy and others have surmised that Col. Gamble, an ardent Federalist, might have harbored some doubts about Wirt's suitability as a son-in-law. One warm summer morning Gamble called early at the young lawyer's office and came across Wirt and several friends still celebrating from the night before. When the Colonel walked in, Wirt stood with his back to the door. Clad only in underwear with a wash basin on his head and brandishing a fireplace poker and sheet iron blower, Wirt was engaged in a dramatic presentation of "Falstaff's onset upon the thieves." The opening of the door drew everyone's attention. After a moment's hesitation, Col. Gamble gave his future son-in-law an ironic bow and departed without a word.[8]

In what was perhaps an attempt to elevate his flagging esteem in the eyes of Col. Gamble, Wirt accepted the next honor that was thrust upon him by his supportive friends. From 1778, civil and property matters in Virginia had been adjudicated by a single Chancellor, a post held all that time by the venerable George Wythe. But in 1802 the General Assembly decided the case load had grown too large for even one of Wythe's abilities. The Commonwealth was divided into three Chancery districts. Wirt was appointed to be judge of the Tidewater District, which encompassed all of Virginia southeast of Richmond, including the Eastern Shore, the old capital of Williamsburg and the thriving ports of Norfolk and Hampton. Considering Wythe's formidable reputation and Wirt's relative inexperience, it was a weighty honor – so much so, in fact, that Wirt had a hard time believing it. At first he refused to leave the hall before the vote was taken, not understanding why the clerk should not be present. After he returned and was informed that he had been selected unanimously, Wirt still had some questions about his qualifications for the job. He called upon the Governor to express these doubts. Monroe, it is said, replied that the Legislature "knew very well what it was doing, and that it was not probable he would disappoint either it, or the suitors of the court." Wirt accepted the new position.[9]

In a letter to old friend Dabney Carr, dated Feb. 12, 1802, and posted from Williamsburg, Wirt discussed the mixed feelings he had about relinquishing the duties of Clerk of the House, which he had held through three legislative sessions, and abandoning his new life and law practice in Richmond. This very private letter also hints at its writer's internal battle with a tendency toward life a little bit on the wild side: "There is another reason, *entre nous* I wished to leave Richmond on many accounts. I dropped into a circle dear to me for the amiable and brilliant traits which belonged to it, but in which I had found, that during several months, I was dissipating my health, my time, my money and my reputation. This conviction dwelt so strongly, so incessantly on my mind that all my cheerfulness forsook me, and I awoke many a morning with the feelings of a madman."[10]

The move to Williamsburg did not cool Wirt's relationship with Elizabeth Gamble. On Sept. 7, 1802, they were married in Richmond. Perhaps the self control and personal responsibility he demonstrated in leaving Richmond's night life for the more intellectual atmosphere of Williamsburg and the exacting duties of his new position were sufficient to persuade Elizabeth – and more importantly Col. Gamble – that Wirt was worthy marriage material. Of that there is little doubt. Together they would have twelve children and Wirt, through his letters to Elizabeth over the next three decades, would continue to demonstrate his affection for the merchant's daughter. Wirt moved his new wife to Williamsburg in November and spent the winter applying himself to the duties of the Chancellor's office.

But the constraints of providing for a wife and household on a limited salary and Wirt's restless nature soon had him dreaming of greener pastures. At first he thought about picking up and moving westward to Kentucky, which he saw as a rugged new land of opportunity. Friends who had gone west urged him to come, assuring him that a lawyer there could make considerably more than he did in Virginia. In a letter to Dabney Carr dated February, 13, 1803, Wirt detailed his disenchantment with the structured position in which he found himself and romanticized about the allure of life beyond the Appalachian Mountains: "This honor of being a Chancellor is a very empty thing, stomachically speaking; that is, although a man be full of honor, his stomach may be empty; or in other words, honor will not go to market and buy a peck of potatoes. On fifteen hundred dollars a year, I can live, but if death comes how will my wife and family live? ...The counsels of my friends in Virginia and in Kentucky, press me with fervor to the latter country. There is an uncommon crisis in the superior courts of that State, and I am very strongly tempted to take advantage of it... Such is the prospect on one hand. On the other, it is possible that I may, like Mr. Wythe, grow old in judicial honors and Roman poverty. I may die beloved, revered almost to canonization by my country, and my wife and children, as they beg for bread, may have to boast that they were mine... If you think it right that I should resign, the questions which remain are, when shall I do so, and in what country shall I resume the practice of law? ... As to this where? In Virginia, the most popular lawyer in the State merely makes the ends of the year meet – I mean Edmund Randolph. I have this from the gentleman who keeps his books. Virginia, therefore, is not the country for my purpose. The federal city is not to my taste or interest. It would require too much time there to take root. In the soil of Kentucky every thing flourishes with rapidity... Pray let me have your thoughts at large on this subject."[11]

During his stay in Williamsburg, Wirt made a number of valuable contacts which brought him additional honors. In 1804, he was appointed to the Board of Visitors of the College of William & Mary.[12] For someone who had only a few years of formal schooling and had never attended college, this honor was a tribute to his growing stature in the literary and legal professions.

Chapter 6

Private Practice Resumed

Wirt struggled with his decision through the winter and into the spring of 1803. In the end he rejected the idea of becoming a pioneer in favor of an equally enticing offer to go back into private law practice. Littleton Waller Tazewell persuaded Wirt to grab a share of a lucrative practice in the thriving seaport of Norfolk, a practice that also encompassed Williamsburg and the other areas Wirt had recently become familiar with as Chancellor for the Tidewater District. The offer promised Wirt a ready-made set of clients and the necessary contacts to expand that clientele. One expects that the proximity of his in-laws' home in Richmond also influenced Wirt's decision to stay in Virginia.

Tazewell was two years younger than Wirt, but by 1803 he was already in a position to assist his friend in establishing a new practice. The son of a prominent judge, Tazewell was born in Williamsburg. He received a then-rare Bachelor of Arts degree from the College of William & Mary in 1791. He studied law under Richmond's John Wickham and was licensed to practice in 1796. Tazewell represented James City County in the House of Delegates from 1798 to 1800. In 1800 he was elected to fill out the remainder of John Marshall's term in Congress, serving until March 3, 1801. In 1802, Tazewell moved to Norfolk and began his law practice there, setting up an office at No. 6, Main Street. Tazewell again served in the General Assembly from 1804-1806 and 1816-17. In 1824 he was elected to fill the U.S. Senate seat vacated on the death of John Taylor of Caroline. He was reelected in 1829 and served briefly as President Pro tempore in 1832. In 1834, Tazewell was elected Governor of Virginia, but resigned from that job during the 1836 abolition debate in the General Assembly. He dabbled in politics more than Wirt, but seemed to share his friend's distaste for prolonged service in elected office. Tazewell is described by biographers as an extreme individualist. One can easily imagine how Tazewell and the gregarious and high-spirited Wirt would have become fast friends and collaborators. There were undoubtedly few dull moments in their law offices.

In a letter to Dabney Carr, Wirt pondered the somewhat nomadic existence he had led up to that point in his life and continued to weigh the pros and cons of leaving Virginia. "From the time I first left my native roof (at the age of seven) I have lived nowhere, except merely long enough to let my affections take a firm root, when, either want or calamity have torn me up, and wafted me into some strange and distant soil. Eight or ten times I have experienced this fate – and although a separation from those whom I love and who love me, however often repeated, would still be painful, I derive comfort from the thought that my stars have never yet thrown me upon a soil too cold or barren for friendship or love... The resignation of the Chancellorship becoming thus inevitable, the only remaining question is, where shall I resume the practice of my profession? ...You ask, why quit the state which has adopted, which has fostered me, which has raised me to its honors? It is the partiality of your friendship which puts this question. I am sure that it is very immaterial to Virginia where I reside."[1]

In another letter to Carr, dated June 6, he announced in a jocular tone: "Well, sir, you have heard that I have disrobed myself of the Chancellor's furs, and I feel much the cooler and lighter for it. Not but that there was some awkwardness in coming down to conflict with men, to whom, a few days before, my dictum was the law. The pride was a false one and I revenged myself on it... You are aware that I am already done with the Kentucky project. I heard, very lately, that there was no *cash* in that state; that fees were paid in horses, cows and sheep, and that the eminence of their lawyers was estimated by the size of their drove, on their return from their circuits: while, on the other hand, I was drawn to Norfolk by the attractions of her bank." Wirt related to Carr a trip to Circuit Court in Suffolk County, where he made $528 in cash and merchandise, "which I consider no ill omen of my future success... Two or three years practice will put me in the possession of cash which, in such a place as Norfolk, I shall be able to turn over to the greatest advantage." [2]

Wirt shed a different light on his decision to choose Norfolk over Kentucky in a letter to former benefactor Benjamin Edwards on March 17, 1805. Edwards was one of the friends who had moved to Kentucky and urged the Wirts to follow: "The first obstacle which I had to encounter arose from the difficulty of compassing so much cash as would enable me to make my debut sufficiently respectable. To have disclosed this obstacle to you or Ninian, after the strong desire which I had manifested to migrate to your state, might have been liable to an interpretation, which, either from true or false pride, I chose to avoid... My wife, who was thoroughly convinced of the propriety of our removal to Kentucky, had consented to it, from the dictates of reason and judgment, whilst her heart and affections secretly revolted against the measure... Waking one night, at midnight, while this journey was contemplated, I found her in tears; and, after much importunity, drew from her an acknowledgment, that her distress proceeded from the idea of such a distant and most probably final separation from her parents and family... Fortune and fame are, indeed, considerations of great weight with me; but they are light, compared with the happiness of the best of wives." [3]

Wirt expressed dismay at the comparatively low salaries of public servants of the day in a letter to another good friend, William Pope of Montpelier, Virginia: "It gives me pleasure to find that my resignation is not disapproved by my friends. To me the measure was indispensably necessary. The present subsistence and future provision of my family depended on it.... To be sure, in a republic, public economy is an important thing; but public justice is still more important; and there is certainly very little justice in expecting the labor and waste of a citizen's life for one-third of the emoluments which he could derive from devoting himself to the service of individuals... It is really humiliating to think, that although these plain truths will be acknowledged by any member of the Legislature to whom you address them in private, yet there is scarcely one man in the House bold enough to vote his sentiments on the subject, after a call of the yeas and nays – he will not dare to jeopard[ize] his re-election by such a vote." In this letter, Wirt also assured Pope that the climate of Norfolk's low-lying environs was not as bad as it was reputed to be and that his law practice there was promising. "I am already engaged in very productive business in five courts... I am very sanguine that, with the blessing of Providence, I shall be able to retire from business in ten or fifteen years, with such a fortune as will place my family, at least above want."[4]

As a precaution, Elizabeth Wirt, who was with child, stayed in Richmond during the summer. On September 3, 1803, Wirt became a father, Elizabeth giving birth to a baby girl they named Laura Henrietta – the first of twelve children. Wirt's own youth was made tragic by the loss of his mother and father. His first marriage, shortened by his wife's premature death, was childless. Wirt was ecstatic about becoming a father. Although cases in far-flung courtrooms often kept him away from home, his frequent letters to Elizabeth left little doubt about his devotion to her and his growing family: "How rugged would the path even of duty appear; how fruitless, how solitary, how disconsolate would even prosperity be, if I alone were to taste it! It is the thought that my wife and children are to share it with me ... These are the fond ideas which possess my soul, which never fail to smooth my brow in the midst of tumult, to speak peace to my heart, and to scatter roses over my path of life."[5] Wirt also confided in Elizabeth about his struggle to reconcile a strong sense of faith and social responsibility with his weaknesses toward drink and merriment: "I must confess that the natural gaiety of my character, rendered still more reckless by the dissipation into which I had been allured, had sealed my eyes, and hidden from me the rich inheritance of the righteous. It was you, whose example and tender exhortations rescued me from the horrors of confirmed guilt, and taught me once more to raise my suppliant mind to God. The more I reflect on it, the more highly do I prize this obligation... How should I be laughed at if this letter were read by those who once were my wild companions! How should I be envied if they knew the sweet feelings with which I have poured out these reflections, warm from my heart."[6]

About four months after he announced his return to private practice, Wirt and Tazewell defended a client named Shannon, who was charged with murder. It was a performance Wirt thought worthy of retelling at a later date. Shannon's father-in-law had been killed in his own home in Williamsburg, shot through the window by an unknown assailant with a shotgun. The next morning, neighbors attempted to reenact the crime and discovered a small piece of paper that apparently had been used as wadding in the shotgun. The scrap of paper bore the letter "*m*" upon it and looked as if it had been torn from a piece of correspondence. When someone remarked that it was curious that Shannon had not come to his father-in-law's house that morning to help with the investigation, a search was launched. They found him, not at his home on the other side of the James River, but asleep at a tavern 30 miles away. Further inquiry revealed that Shannon had been in Williamsburg on the day of the murder and that he had asked a blacksmith to repair his shotgun. Because the repair could not be made on the spot, Shannon took the gun with him. After his arrest, Shannon was found to have buckshot on him, as well as a letter missing a corner, which appeared to match the scrap of wadding found at the scene of the crime. Armed with a solid circumstantial case, the Commonwealth went to trial only to come up against Wirt and company, who bedazzled the jury and a packed courthouse with their eloquent defense. One juror refused to agree to a guilty finding and Shannon was set free. In a letter written to his wife during the course of the trial, Wirt hinted of his client's roguish demeanor: "What do you think of Shannon's gallantry? Although in irons and chained to the wall and floor, he has made a conquest of the gaoler's wife, and she has declared her resolution to petition for a divorce from her husband, and follow Shannon, if he is acquitted, to the end of the world."[7]

In December, three months after the birth of their first child, the Wirts moved their household to Norfolk, where they would reside for two years. Rebuilt from smoldering ruins after the British bombardment on January 1, 1776, and subsequent torching by misguided patriots, Norfolk was, in 1804, a bustling seaport town with a population of more than 9,000 residents. Because of war in Europe, American trade to the West Indies boomed, jumping from $2.1 million in 1792 to $9.7 million in 1801. Much of this was routed through the seaports of Hampton Roads. The number of foreign vessels to enter the Port of Norfolk rose from 356 in 1800 to 484 in 1803. In 1806, Norfolk's merchants owned 120 vessels, aggregating 23,207 tons, used exclusively in foreign trade.[8] To an ambitious lawyer, the seaport boasted an abundance of criminal matters and commercial and maritime law. A total stranger to maritime law on his arrival in Norfolk, Wirt busily applied himself to filling in this gap in his resume. "In the Borough of Norfolk every drone feels the pressure of business," Wirt wrote to Carr in June, 1804. "This pressure, too often, depends less on the quantum of business than on the strength and dexterity of the agent. If I had given more of my time to the books and practice of my profession, I should have less investigation and toil to undergo now... The consequence is, that being transplanted to the shores of the Atlantic, where the questions grow almost entirely out of commerce, I have fallen into a business totally new to me, and every case calls for elaborate examination."[9]

Although there was plenty of business in Norfolk, the seaport town lacked the polish and sophistication to which the Wirts were accustomed. La Rochefoucauld observed after his visit to Norfolk in 1796: "It is one of the ugliest, most irregular, dirtiest towns that I have ever seen. The houses are low and mean, almost all of wood, ... not twenty being of brick. The streets are unpaved; the town is surrounded by a marsh."[10] It is doubtful that conditions were much improved by 1803. In the alleys leading from Water Street to Main, there were many "filthy, tobacco-impregnated barrooms," and "licentious dance cellars." One night in 1803, bands of drunken sailors rioted in the streets, injuring many people with stones. One unfortunate soul had his neck nearly severed from a stroke with a shingle, reported the Norfolk *Herald* on July 18, 1803.[11] In 1799, many buildings on the east side of Market Square were destroyed by fire. On Feb. 22, 1804, a second fire destroyed over 300 warehouses, stores and houses. Several ships caught fire, drifted out into the harbor and set additional ships ablaze. "Indeed, it was a most awful sight to see, the columns of smoke, the bursting out of the flames, the cries of those that were on the streets saving their little properties, exposed to a most terrible, drifty and snowing night" observed William Couper in a letter dated April 27, 1804.[12] A third fire in 1805 destroyed 10 or 12 houses on Water Street. In 1806, Thomas Moore said this about a visit to Norfolk: "At the time we arrived, the yellow fever had not disappeared, and every odor that assailed us in the streets, accounted very strongly for its visitation." The best thing that could be said about Norfolk, The Norfolk *Gazette and Public Ledger* quoted Moore as saying, was that it "abounds in dogs, negroes, and in democrats." [13]

Wirt complained, during his stay in Norfolk, about the high prices he found in the waterfront boom town: "Norfolk is very expensive. I keep a pair of horses here which cost me eight pounds [$40] per month. Wood is four to eight dollars per cord; Indian meal, through the winter, is nine shillings per bushel; flour, eleven and twelve dollars per barrel; a leg of mutton, three dollars; butter, three shillings per pound; eggs, two shillings and three pence per dozen, and so on."[14]

On January 31, 1805, a day after her 21st birthday, Elizabeth Wirt gave birth to a son, whom they named Robert Gamble Wirt, in honor of her father. Wirt, then 32, described his first son as, "certainly a very handsome child, and if there be any truth in physiognomy, a fellow whose native sheet of intellectual paper, is of as fine a texture and as lustrous a white, as the fond heart even of a parent can desire. My fancy is already beginning to build for him some of those airy tenements, in the erection of which, my youth has been wasted... I hope we may reach my wished for number of twelve, and be almost as patriarchal, by and by, as yourself," Wirt wrote Benjamin Edwards.[15]

Although business was good, the high prices, shoddy appearance of all but Norfolk's better residential areas, constant threat of fire and periodic worry about yellow fever must have weighed heavily on Wirt, his wife and two young children. Betsy Wirt, who never left Richmond in her heart, lobbied her husband to move their household back to the Capital, once calling her life in Norfolk a "misery." She intensified this effort after her sister's marriage to William H. Cabell in the spring of 1805, and his election as Governor in the fall.[16] On May 10, 1805, Wirt wrote to his wife, "We will go to Richmond to live as soon as prudence will permit. But Norfolk is the ladder by which we are to climb the hills of Richmond advantageously – Norfolk is the cradle of our fortune." In April, 1806, Wirt wrote his wife from Williamsburg, saying, "I told the Judge [Tucker] privately, that my friends were pressing me to fix myself in Richmond. He caught at it with his usual enthusiasm – insisted that I should adopt this plan – swore that I could not *live* another year in Norfolk – declared that I had fattened at least forty pounds since he saw me in the winter, and that I was so fit a subject for the fever, he didn't know the man on whose life he would not sooner buy an annuity than on mine: said he was sure I should do well at the bar there, after a year or two..."[17] In the August 8, 1806, edition of the Norfolk *Public Ledger*, Wirt announced the following:

> *Apprehensions for the health of his family, having induced the subscriber, very reluctantly, to remove from the Borough of Norfolk, he has fixed his final residence in Richmond, and may be found always at his office near the capitol, in the house lately occupied by M. Jones, Esq. the Commissioner of Loans. He proposes to practice law in the Federal Courts, Court of Appeals, and Chancery Court in Richmond, and will also continue to practice in the Chancery Court at Williamsburg and District Court of Suffolk. His clients in the County and Borough Courts of Norfolk, are referred to Messrs. Littleton W. Tazewell and Robert B. Taylor, who have obligingly undertaken to finish his business there – in all important cases, in which those gentlemen have been previously engaged, or where the partiality of a client may have relied peculiarly on the subscriber, he will continue to give his attendance.[18]*

Chapter 7

The 'British Spy'

Shortly before moving his family to Norfolk, William Wirt served notice of his literary pretensions. He penned a series of essays which ran in *The Argus* of Richmond, a Jeffersonian Republican newspaper, in September and October, 1803, and which came to be known as *The Letters of the British Spy*. These essays appeared anonymously, under the guise of an Englishman writing home his observations of American society and the political and civic leadership of Virginia. Wirt's authorship was soon ferreted out. The essays became a runaway success and were republished many times. The tenth edition, published in 1832 by Harpers & Brothers, contains Peter Hoffman Cruse's 82-page biographical sketch, the only substantive biography of Wirt written during his lifetime.

In the lighthearted tone that characterized many of his letters, Wirt wrote Dabney Carr from Norfolk, on January 16, 1804, about his literary phenomenon: "I come, in order, to a certain author *y'clept* the British Spy. I shall not be either so unfriendly or so childishly affected as to deny the brat to be my own... The *thing* is as generally and confidently imputed to me, as if my name were in the title page. For you are to understand that, very far beyond my expectations, the printer has found it in his interest not only to bind it up in a pamphlet, but to issue a second edition." Wirt confessed to his friend that he began to write the essays "to divert my own mind," but warmed up to the subject and was encouraged by friends and by his wife, who read them and liked them. "I adopted the character of a British Spy, because I thought that such a title, in a Republican paper, would excite more attention, curiosity and interest than any other... I endeavored to forget myself; to fancy myself the character which I had assumed; to imagine how, as a Briton, I should be struck with Richmond, its landscapes, its public characters, its manners, together with the political sentiments and moral complexion of the Virginians generally. I succeeded so well that in several parts of the country, particularly in Gloucester, and in the neighborhood of Norfolk, the people went so far as to declare that they had seen the very foreigner (and a Briton he was, too), who had written the letters." The editor of a newspaper in Massachusetts, who reprinted the letters, declared them written by an American educated abroad, Wirt noted.[1]

Although immensely popular with the public, Wirt's characterizations of some Virginians, though he referred to no one by name, hit a little too close for comfort – especially with Edmund Randolph and John Wickham, two very prominent attorneys. *The Spy* described Randolph as, "large and portly... his mind, as is often but not invariably the case, corresponds with his personal appearance: that is, that it is turned rather for ornament than for severe use."[2] Wirt observed after its publication, "I forgot myself too far in some of the letters... hence the portraits of living characters, which I drew with a mind as perfectly absorbed in the contemplation of the originals, and as *forgettive* of personal consequences 'as if I had really belonged to another planet;' and upon my honor, with as little ill-will towards either of the gentlemen. It was not until it appeared in print that the letter portraying R— and W— [Randolph and Wickham] startled me. Then the indiscretion stared me full in the face; but 'the die was cast' – and to make the worst of it, I had merely published imprudent truths. But I had made enemies of the gentlemen themselves, with all their connexions and dependencies."

Randolph, Wirt added, told George Wythe that he wished "the British Spy was practicing at that bar." When they later met in court in Suffolk, Wirt said, Randolph was still miffed. Fearing that the animosity might jeopardize his case, Wirt said he attempted to make light of the schism. "I had, however, no intention to wound his feelings, but merely to do justice to my cause, and give it a fair play before the court... he professed to be satisfied; but he was disconcerted and wounded, past all power of forgiving. He was so confounded, that in his argument he manifested nothing of the orator, nor even of himself, but the person and voice. His arguments were the very weakest his cause furnished; his order (to use an Irishism) was all confusion, and he is said to have made the very worst speech that he ever did make. In short, he disappointed every body, and lost a cause which he had declared himself, all over the country, sure to gain. If he had never been my enemy before, that one adventure would have made him so." Wickham, Wirt said, was more forgiving. "Mr. W— is not only reconciled, but to all appearance, even partial to me, since he has been lately instrumental in promoting my professional benefit," Wirt wrote Carr. "Marshall, too, has given me a fee in a Chancery case... I am sure I am no libeler in intention; and if I am not blinded by partiality, the portraits in question are marked with candor and benevolence... I am not yet convinced that established lawyers are not proper game for the press, *so far as concerns their talents*; nor am I clear that the procedure was wrong on the ground of public utility. That it was indiscreet, I am willing to admit, and I heartily wish I had let them alone."[3]

Wirt's artful weaving of "candor and benevolence" can be seen in his sensitive portrait of James Monroe, a friend, benefactor and, shortly before *The Spy* was being written, Governor of Virginia: "His dress and personal appearance are those of a plain and modest gentleman. He is a man of soft, polite and even assiduous attentions... there is often in his manner an artificial and even an awkward simplicity, which while it provokes the smile of a more polished person, forces him to the opinion that Mr. — is a man of a most sincere and artless soul. Nature has given him a mind neither rapid nor rich; and therefore, he cannot shine on a subject which is entirely new to him. But to compensate him for this, he is endued *(sic)* with a spirit of generous and restless emulation, a judgment solid, strong and clear, and a habit of application, which no difficulties can shake; no labours can tire... his sober steady and faithful judgment has saved him from the common error of more quick and brilliant geniuses; the too hasty adoption of specious, but false conclusions. These qualities render him a safe and an able counselor. And by their constant exertion, he has amassed a store of knowledge, which having passed seven times through the crucible, is almost as highly corrected as human knowledge can be; and which certainly may be much more safely relied on than the spontaneous and luxuriant growth of a more fertile, but less chastened mind..."[4] Although he was stung by Wirt's somewhat unflattering portrayal, Monroe never let it get in the way of their friendship.

Letter I of *The Spy* provided a colorful description of the town of Richmond in 1803: "Richmond occupies a very picturesque and most beautiful situation. I have never met with such an assemblage of striking and interesting objects. The town, dispersed over hills of various shapes; the river descending from west to east, and obstructed by a multitude of small islands, clumps of trees, and myriads of rocks; among which it tumbles, foams, and roars, constituting what are called the falls; the same river, at the lower end of town, bending at right angles to the south, and winding reluctantly off for many miles... its polished surface caught here and there by the eye, but more generally covered from the view by trees; among which the white sails of approaching and departing vessels exhibit a curious and interesting appearance: then again, on the opposite side, the little town of Manchester, built on a hill, which sloping gently to the river, opens the whole town to the view, interspersed, as it is, with vigorous, and flourishing poplars, and surrounded to a great distance by green plains and stately woods – all these objects, falling at once under the eye, constitute, by far, the most finely varied and most animated landscape that I have ever seen."[5]

In Letter IV, *The Spy* discusses the plight of Native Americans after a visit to a farm built over the village in which "Pocahuntas" *(sic)* once lived. Although written from the standpoint of a European visitor, this letter reveals much about Wirt's attitude toward the plight of the land's original inhabitants:

"The people here may say what they please; but, on the principles of eternal truth and justice, they have no right to this country. They say that they have bought it – bought it! Yes – of whom? Of the poor trembling natives who knew that refusal would be in vain; and who strove to make a merit of necessity by seeming to yield with grace, what they knew that they had not the power to retain... Poor wretches! No wonder that they are so implacably vindictive against the white people; no wonder that the rage of resentment is handed down from generation to generation... Make them forget, too, if you can, that in the midst of all this innocence, simplicity and bliss – the white man came, and lo! – the animated chase, the feast, the dance, the song of fearless, thoughtless joy were over; that ever since, they have been made to drink of the bitter cup of humiliation; treated like dogs... until, driven from river to river, from forest to forest, and through a period of two hundred years, rolled back nation upon nation, they find themselves fugitives, vagrants and strangers in their own country, and look forward to the certain period when their descendants will be totally extinguished by wars, driven at the point of the bayonet into the western ocean, or reduced to a fate still more deplorable and horrid, the condition of slaves."[6]

Wirt's admiration for accomplished orators and his underlying faith in a supreme being are reflected in Letter VII, in which he recounts entering "a ruinous, old, wooden house in the forest, not far from the roadside" and listening to a sermon about the Crucifixion by James Waddell, the "Blind Preacher" of Orange County, Virginia:

"On entering, I was struck with his preternatural appearance, he was a tall and very spare old man; his head, which was covered with a white linen cap, his shriveled hands, and his voice, were all shaking under the influence of a palsy; and a few moments ascertained to me that he was perfectly blind. The first emotions which touched my breast were those of mingled pity and veneration. But ah! sacred God! How soon were all my feelings changed... His enunciation was so deliberate, that his voice trembled on every syllable; and every heart in the assembly trembled in unison... We saw the very faces of the Jews: the staring, frightful distortions of malice and rage... when he came to touch on the patience, the forgiving meekness of our Saviour; when he drew, to the life, his blessed eyes streaming in tears to heaven; his voice breathing to God, a soft and gentle prayer of pardon on his enemies, 'Father, forgive them, for they know not what they do' – the voice of the preacher, which had all along faltered, grew fainter and fainter, until his utterance being entirely obstructed by the force of his feelings, he raised his handkerchief to his eyes, and burst into a loud and irrepressible flood of grief. The effect is inconceivable. The whole house resounded with the mingled groans, and sobs, and shrieks of the congregation... The first sentence, with which he broke the awful silence, was a quotation from Rousseau, 'Socrates died like a philosopher, but Jesus Christ like a God!' ...Never before, did I completely understand what Demosthenes meant by laying such stress on *delivery*... If he had been indeed and in truth an angel of light, the effect could scarcely have been more divine... This man has been before my imagination almost ever since. A thousand times, as I rode along, I dropped the reins of my bridle, stretched forth my hand, and tried to imitate his quotation from Rousseau; a thousand times I abandoned the attempt in despair, and felt persuaded that his peculiar manner and power arose from an energy of soul, which nature could give, but which no human being could copy."[7]

Duke University Professor Jay B. Hubbell examined the newspaper essays penned by Wirt and his cronies (*Letters of a British Spy*, 1803; *Rainbow*, 1804, and *The Old Bachelor*, 1814) in "William Wirt and the Familiar Essay in Virginia." He concluded that, although not a literary giant, "In those days, however, Wirt had few able competitors in the field of American Literature. Of the two "Rainbow" series, Hubbell said, "The great majority of the essays are thoughtful, intelligent, and for the most part competently written." Noting that the first southern literary magazine, the *Southern Literary Messenger,* did not come along until 1834, the year Wirt died, Hubbell concluded that Wirt's newspaper essays occupy a unique place in literature, and well represent Wirt's stated intent: "virtuously to instruct, or innocently to amuse."[8]   In "William Wirt and the Legend of the Old South," Harvard Professor William Robert Taylor pointed out that Wirt's essays and his later biography were written not by a man who devoted his entire life to literature but by a busy, upwardly mobile lawyer who wrote as a means of being known. "Wirt himself compared writing a book to throwing a stone into a mill pond. His earlier writing, he said, barely made a ripple. To succeed, he felt it would be necessary to make a splash."[9]

In a letter to Benjamin Edwards, Wirt admits as much, saying that he wrote all of "The Letters of The British Spy" to "while away six anxious weeks which preceded the birth of my daughter... It has been the means of making me extensively known, and known to my advantage, except, perhaps, with such men as Jefferson and Jay, whose just minds readily ascertain the difference between bullion and chaff." Although his later essays achieved some popularity, none rivaled that of *The Spy.*[10]   His fling at biography many years later was a popular hit, but panned by critics. Throughout his life, Wirt would lament the fact that the necessity of making a living prevented him from more assiduously pursuing the craft of writing.

Chapter 8

The George Wythe Murder Case

It would take Wirt less than the predicted two years to reestablish himself in Virginia's capital. Two high-profile cases would make the young lawyer's name a household word and elevate him to the ranks of the top lawyers in the Commonwealth.

The first of these cases was one he mulled over for some time before accepting. George Wythe, the venerable Chancellor, died in Richmond on June 8, 1806 under somewhat mysterious circumstances. Although he was 80, there was suspicion of foul play. Wythe had lived alone in his later years, with the exception of his sister's teenage grandson, George Wythe Swinney (or Sweeney) who moved in for a time and was expected to inherit a generous portion of Wythe's estate. Based on the common belief that Swinney tried to hurry up his uncle's demise, perhaps by slipping arsenic in his coffee, the younger man was charged with murder.

Swinney asked Wirt to defend him. The lawyer had serious misgivings about accepting the fee, seeking the counsel of his wife and Judge William Nelson, whom Wirt contacted while trying a case in Williamsburg. Nelson was kin to Wythe's second wife, who was a Taliaferro. "I dare say you have heard me say that I hoped no one would undertake the defense of Swinney, but that he would be left to the fate which he seemed so justly to merit," Wirt wrote his wife. "Judge Nelson, himself, has changed, a good deal, the course of my opinions on this subject, by stating that there was a difference. in the opinion of the faculty in Richmond as to the cause of Mr. Wythe's death... I had concluded that his innocence was possible, and, therefore, that it would not be so horrible a thing to defend him as, at first, I had thought it." Further persuasion came in the form of another of Swinney's uncles who told Wirt that the young man's mother was distraught over her son's plight. Wirt promised Swinney's relatives he would consider the case and come to a decision within a month. He conferred further with his wife before accepting the case, "to my own heart I mean to stand justified by doing nothing that I think wrong. But for your sakes, I wish to do nothing that the *world* shall think wrong," he wrote his wife. After considerable deliberation, Wirt agreed to join Edmund Randolph in Swinney's defense.[1]

There was considerable evidence against young Swinney, although most of it was circumstantial in nature. Wythe's cook said she had seen the nephew come into the kitchen and drop a white substance into the coffee pot, and that he had made an excuse when he realized he had been seen. The cook and a mulatto boy whom the elder Wythe had taken under his roof also drank some of the coffee and the boy, Michael Brown, preceded Wythe to the great beyond by several days. The suspect coffee grounds were thrown into the trash heap and some chickens that feasted on these coffee grounds also reportedly died. Wythe, however, lived long enough after drinking the coffee to write Swinney out of his will.

George Wythe's death shocked his many friends, most of whom were quick to condemn Swinney, who, although he was but 17, had already gained an unsavory reputation for drinking and gambling. President Thomas Jefferson, who studied under Wythe at the College of William and Mary, declared him "the best Latin and Greek Scholar in the State." Wythe was also one of the young nation's foremost legal scholars, creating a good portion of Virginia's legal system when the colonies broke away from England. Jefferson branded Swinney's alleged act, "such an instance of depravity [as] has been hitherto known to us only in the fables of the poets."[2] Wirt also was indignant about "the dose of arsenick *(sic)* administered" to "poor old Chancellor Wythe... The chain of circumstances fix the quilt of Sweney (sic) beyond the reach of doubt," Wirt opined to James Monroe just two days after Wythe died. Always the lawyer, however, Wirt quickly grasped a possible line of defense. In his letter to Monroe, he added, "But some of those circumstances, material to his conviction in a court of law, depend, it seems, on black persons, and so he will escape for the poison[ings]. He is under prosecution for the forgery and of that must be convicted."[3]

Very little accurate information survives on the murder trial of George Wythe Swinney, which took place on Sept. 1, 1806. None of the prinicpals wrote about it to any extent and the court records, apparently, did not survive the Confederate evacuation of Richmond in April, 1865. Surviving accounts written by several men on the periphery of the case are highly opinionated and were not penned until several decades after

Wythe's death. Scholars W. Edwin Hemphill and Julian P. Boyd were able to reconstruct the evidence against Swinney through these accounts, newspaper reports and the complete lower court records, where Swinney was arraigned on June 26, 1806. Hemphill and Boyd surmised that much of the evidence presented in the Hustings Court was also presented in the District Court murder trial. That Hemphill and Boyd did not entirely agree in their conclusions, however, is an indication that we don't have the complete picture of Wythe's death and the subsequent trial of Swinney.[4]

Swinney certainly had motive to do away with his aged relative, and even more motive, perhaps, to poison the unfortunate Michael Brown. Wythe, who was a champion of the rights of African-Americans, had taken Brown under his wing and was giving him a classical education as an experiment to prove that blacks were equal in intelligence to whites, given equal environmental circumstances. Wythe's two wives had died before him and he was childless. He was arguably more fond of young Brown than his sybaritic great nephew. Brown was listed as a beneficiary in Wythe's will. The document placed Brown in Thomas Jefferson's care on Wythe's death. It also allocated half of Wythe's bank stock to pay for Brown's upbringing. But the will stated that Brown's share would go to George Wythe Swinney if Brown should "die before his full age." Others listed in the will were Wythe's servants, Lydia Broadnax and Benjamin (no last name), both freed blacks. To Thomas Jefferson, Wythe bequeathed silver cups, a gold-headed cane, books and "philosophical apparatus." Swinney, who was a shameless opportunist, may have reasoned that if Michael Brown died before Wythe, or if they died simultaneously, he, Swinney, would inherit the bulk of the estate.[5]

Swinney was also under some pressure to act. Shortly before the alleged poisonings Swinney had forged George Wythe's name on six checks drawn on the Bank of Virginia. A year previously he had tried to pay off his gambling debts by stealing some of Wythe's books and attempting to sell them at public auction. He was also suspected of selling a prized terrestrial globe that Wythe had intended to leave the more appreciative Jefferson. Wythe was apparently willing to overlook Swinney's earlier indiscretions. But the forged checks might well have overtaxed his avuncular attachment.[6]

This much we do know: On May 25, 1806, which was Whitsunday, George Wythe rose as usual and probably had, as was his custom, a single cup of coffee with a spartan breakfast.

Later that day, Wythe, along with all of the other members of the household except Swinney, became violently ill. Two days later, George Wythe Swinney was arrested and charged with forgery, his great uncle no longer willing, or able, to indulge him. On June 1, 1806, young Michael Brown died. That same day, Wythe revoked all codicils in his will relating to Swinney, and, of course, to Brown, who could no longer benefit from Wythe's generosity. On June 2, the Court of Hustings, which functioned as a semi-permanent grand jury, met at the Courthouse in Richmond and examined Swinney on the forgery charges. They found sufficient evidence to forward the charges to the District Court and set bail at $1,000, no token sum in those days. Wythe lingered on until June 8, when he, too, died.[7]

On June 18, 1806, Swinney was brought before Richmond Mayor Edward Carrington and two other aldermen for a hearing on the charge of murdering Wythe and "Michael Brown the Freed Boy." After five hours, the three officials agreed they were "of Opinion that they, Mr. Wythe & Michael, were poisoned by Geo. W. Sweeney," ordering him to be jailed until the Hustings Court again met on June 23. A parade of witnesses before the Hustings Court testified to Swinney's sudden curiosity about arsenic or ratsbane. William Rose, who lived next door to the jailyard, testified that his servant girl found a packet of arsenic adjacent to the jail wall. Samuel McCraw searched Sweeney's room at Wythe's request and found writing paper that matched the wrapping around the arsenic. He also found a half dozen strawberries that he said appeared to have arsenic sprinkled on them. He said he also found a vial containing what was believed to be a mixture of arsenic and sulfur. McCraw's testimony was corroborated by several other witnesses. Edmund Randolph, the first Attorney General of Virginia, testified that he was summoned to Wythe's bedside on the day Michael Brown died and made requested changes in Wythe's will, leaving the amounts previously bequeathed to Brown and Swinney to Swinney's brothers and sisters. He testified that Wythe told him he had eaten strawberries the evening before he had become ill.[8]

Dr. James McClurg, one of the founders of the Medical Society of Virginia, testified that he was present at the autopsy of Michael Brown's body. The lower part of the stomach was inflamed, consistent with either arsenic poisoning or a large accumulation of bile. McClurg also was present at the autopsy on Wythe, observing bloody intestines and stomach linings. But, McClurg said, if arsenic was involved, death should have occurred sooner than it did. He also testified that Wythe had suffered bowel problems for three years. Dr. James McCaw, Wythe's attending physician, said he visited Wythe on May 26, after Wythe had experienced violent bouts of vomiting and purging. Dr. McCaw administered an opiate and Wythe's condition improved somewhat, he said, but went into a steady decline the following day, after news of Swinney's arrest. McCaw was also at the autopsy and ascribed the cause of death as excess bile. Dr. William Foushee, another attendee at the autopsy, which apparently drew most of Richmond's medical community, observed an inflamed stomach condition which might have been produced by arsenic or an acrid substance.[9]

Although Wythe's cook, Lydia Broadnax, told investigators that she saw Swinney place a white substance in the coffee pot on the morning of May 25, her testimony apparently was disallowed at both the preliminary hearing and the murder trial because of the Virginia statute limiting the admissibility of a black's testimony against a white defendant. Without this evidence, as Wirt correctly surmised, the state's case was a weak one of circumstantial evidence. And with the conflicting testimony of the doctors who observed Wythe and attended the autopsy, it would have been difficult to even establish, beyond a reasonable doubt, that Wythe was poisoned. Also missing from the murder trial, presumably, was Edmund Randolph's testimony. Inexplicably, the eminent lawyer appeared as Wirt's co-counsel for the defense. Based on the circumstantial nature of the evidence, Wirt and Randolph won an acquittal for Swinney. The Richmond *Enquirer* reported that after a day-long "able and eloquent discussion, the jury retired, and in a few minutes, brought in a verdict of not guilty." The second murder indictment for the death of Michael Brown was withdrawn by Phillip N. Nicholas, the state's Attorney General, who figured that with his lack of success on Wythe's death, he would do no better with Brown's.[10]

On the following day, Swinney was tried and convicted on two of the six counts of forgery. Swinney was sentenced to six months in jail and one hour of humiliation on the pillory at Richmond's market house. Wirt immediately lodged an appeal for arrest of judgment, which was heard ten days later. Wirt's arguments met with favor from Judges Prentiss and Tyler of the District Court, and the matter was set to the next session of General Court. Wirt argued that Swinney's forgeries did not constitute an offense under the law of 1789 cited at trial. The law was "intended to punish a pre-existing evil," Wirt contended. But it could not have any reference to the Bank of

Virginia, established after the 1789 law was passed. The law also applied to the robbery of "private individuals," and the bank could not be construed to be a "person or persons" within the letter of the law. The bank was "no more a person, than the commonwealth of Virginia," Wirt continued. He also argued that what funds Swinney had received were not the property of George Wythe because they were delivered under a check not drawn by him and the bank had no right to charge Wythe's account. Swinney had committed a forgery, but under the laws of the day, it was not an illegal forgery. The judges agreed with this, but they did not agree that the Bank could not withdraw the funds from Wythe's account. With Wirt greasing the skids, Swinney slid through a loophole in the law.[11]

Although indignant about Swinney escaping punishment, the local press praised Wirt's performance. The Virginia *Gazette & General Advertiser* said Wirt delivered "an eloquent and ingenious speech." The General Assembly was alerted to the loophole Swinney slipped through and closed it. On the last day of the year, the legislators met to adopt "An ACT to punish certain thefts and forgeries," which defined as a criminal act every deed which allowed someone to "fraudulently obtain, or aid or assist in obtaining from the Bank of Virginia, or any of its offices of discount or deposit, any bank note, or money, by means of any forged or counterfeited check or order whatsoever, knowing the same to be forged or counterfeited." The penalty was set at "not less than two, nor more than ten years." It took much longer to change the statute that prohibited blacks from testifying against whites. That law was not repealed until 1867.[12]

Despite his successes in criminal court, Wirt confessed that he did not enjoy getting miscreants off the hook, especially in trials that took him away from home and hearth. "I look to you as a refuge from care and toil," he wrote his wife. "It is this anticipation only which enables me to sustain the pressure of employment so uncongenial with my spirit: this indiscriminate defense of right and wrong – this zealous advocation of causes at which my soul revolts – this playing of the nurse to villains, and occupying myself continually in cleansing them – it is sickening, even to death. But the time will come when I hope it will be unnecessary."[13]

Chapter 9

The Burr Treason Trial

W irt's next major case cast him in the unaccustomed role of prosecutor, although there were indications that his services had also been sought by the defendant. Unlike today's media, newspapers of Wirt's day did not trumpet cases as "The Trial of the Century;" besides, the century was but six years old in 1807. Had they such proclivities, however, the trial of former Vice President Aaron Burr on charges of treason would certainly have been a likely candidate. It was, by far, the biggest case to come along in Wirt's 15 years of practicing law. A lawyer and distinguished Revolutionary War officer, Burr was the Federalist Party's presidential nominee in 1800, achieving a tie with Jefferson in electoral votes (73-73). On the 36th ballot, the House of Representatives selected Jefferson, President and Burr, Vice President. The relationship was a stormy one. Burr faded from politics after the duel in which he killed Alexander Hamilton and became involved in a variety of intrigues on the western frontier. These included stillborn schemes to seize New Orleans, invade Mexico and create a new nation in the southwest that he would rule as emperor.

In January, 1807, Burr was arrested on the Mississippi River, escaped custody and was again arrested at Fort Stoddard, near Mobile. He was transported to Richmond to be tried for high treason for conspiring to levy war against the United States on Dec. 10, 1806, and the additional misdemeanor of planning an invasion of Spanish territories. He arrived in Richmond on March 26 and was arraigned before Chief Justice John Marshall, a staunch Federalist, on March 30. The first day of the arraignment was held in the Eagle Tavern in Richmond. On the second day, the proceedings were moved to the General Assembly to accommodate the huge throng.

Burr hired some of the finest legal minds to defend him against what he contended to be trumped up and politically motivated charges. His defense team consisted of Edmund Randolph, U.S. Attorney General under George Washington;

John Wickham, the most versatile lawyer at the Virginia Bar (both Randolph and Wickham were targets of "The British Spy's" satirical pen); Benjamin Botts, a young lawyer with a Scottish wit; Jack Baker, who walked with a crutch and was adept at clowning for the crowd; Charles Lee and Luther Martin, a Jefferson foe from Maryland. Aligned against this "dream team" was George Hay, the U.S. Attorney for Virginia and Monroe's son-in-law; Virginia Lt. Gov. Alexander MacRae and Wirt. Much of the prosecution's strategy would come by mail from Jefferson.

Fearing that Hay and MacRae lacked the brilliance necessary to cope with Burr's stellar defense team, aided and abetted by Marshall, the presiding judge and no friend of the President, Jefferson insisted that Hay retain Wirt. Federal Judge Thomas Rodney (a Jefferson appointee and father of Attorney General Caesar Rodney) instructed Hay to hire "two of the ablest available counsel." His first choice was Wickham, but Burr had already retained him, along with Edmund Randolph, another recommendation. Rodney reported to Jefferson that Burr had also written Phillip Norborne Nicholas, who refused to see him, and sought the services of Wirt, who was out of town trying a case in Williamsburg at the time. Thus forewarned, Hay was able to contact "that eloquent young man [Wirt] and gained his services for the prosecution."[1]   Although much of the prosecution's case was eroded by Marshall's partisan rulings on what evidence could be submitted to the jury, the opportunity to butt heads with some of the finest legal talent in a nationally publicized trial was a win-win situation for Wirt.

Marshall refused to directly indict Burr, freeing the defendant on his own recognizance to socialize with Richmond's Federalist elite while awaiting a grand jury. At one dinner party, hosted by John Wickham, both Burr and Marshall were invited in what Wickham termed an oversight. The accused, the judge and the defense lawyer dined genially. The grand jury, which convened on May 22 had John Randolph of Roanoke as its foreman and included a future Secretary of War, and several senators-and governors-to-be. Outside the state house, Gen. Andrew Jackson inflamed the crowd on the capital green, denouncing Jefferson's "political persecution" of Burr. Young Washington Irving was sent to cover the proceedings for a New York newspaper. Thousands of supporters and enemies of Burr's thronged to Richmond to become part of the spectacle, filling all available rooms and setting up campsites in and around the city. After a number of delays, including one, according to Irving, to allow the jurors to "go home, see their wives, get their clothes washed and flog their negroes," the grand jury on June 24 brought in indictments for treason against Col. Burr and his alleged co-conspirators Harman Blennerhassett, Jonathan Dayton, John Smith, Comfort Tyler, Israel Smith and Davis Floyd.[2]

After spending two nights in jail, Burr was allowed to lodge with one of his lawyers, Luther Martin. But when the trial was postponed until August 3, Burr was provided with three "good-sized rooms" at the state penitentiary a mile outside town. The only reason, Irving wrote, "for immuring (sic) him in this abode of thieves, cut-throats and incendiaries," was to save the state money and "insure (sic) the security of the person." Incarceration did not much alter Burr's lifestyle. Blennerhassett complained that it was difficult for him to get an audience with Burr, "as if he really were an Emperor," because people swamped him with "messages, notes and inquiries, bringing oranges, lemons, pineapples, raspberries, apricots, cream, butter, ice and some ordinary articles..." and that his secretary drove out daily from town, "freighted with cake, confectionery, flowers, redolent with perfume, wreathed into fancy bouquets of endless variety."[3] Wirt's mother-in-law, Mrs. Gamble, sent Blennerhassett fruit and calf's-foot jelly packed in ice. Wirt's brother-in-law, John Gamble, acted as one of Burr's securities. Col. Gamble was outspoken in his opinion that Burr's prosecution was a manifestation of Jefferson's jealousy toward Burr, which must have made for tense moments around the Gamble-Wirt dinner table that year.

During the delay before trial, the state's star witness, Army General James Wilkinson, was not doing the prosecution's case much good, according to Irving, by swaggering drunkenly from tavern-to-tavern, wearing a Turkish sash and oversized white hat, and placing wagers on the prisoner's eventual conviction. Irving, who it must be remembered represented the Federalist press from Burr's hometown, described Wilkinson on the stand as "obese, grandiloquent – strutting and swelling like a turkey cock."[5]

Richmond was in the midst of a heat wave, the thermometer hovering in the high 90s, when the trial finally started on August 3, 1807. A noisy throng milled outside the courtroom in the hot sun, while those fortunate enough to gain entrance jammed the House of Delegates gallery in equal discomfort. Young Winfield Scott stood on the big lock on the front door to catch a glimpse of the spectacle within. Burr appeared in court on the arm of his reluctant son-in-law, who had been coaxed out of his refuge in South Carolina for a show of family solidarity – but not before having first written Governor Pinckney in an attempt to exonerate himself from any knowledge of, or participation in, his notorious father-in-law's projects.[6]

Wirt's most memorable role in the trial was his delivery of a four-hour oration in answer to a defense motion that the charges against Burr be dropped because he was not present on Blennerhassett's island in the Ohio River at the time it was raided, and that, as a consequence, could not be regarded as a full-fledged participant in the treasonable rebellion. Excerpts of that speech are as follows:

"...Let us compare the two men and settle this question of precedence between them. It may save a good deal of troublesome ceremony hereafter... Who Aaron Burr is, we have seen, in part, already. I will add, that beginning his operations in New York, he associates with him men to supply the necessary funds. Possessed of the main spring, his personal labor contrives all the machinery. Pervading the continent from New York to New Orleans, he draws into his plan, by every allurement which he can contrive, men of all ranks and descriptions... All this his restless ambition has contrived; and in the autumn of 1806, he goes forth, for the last time, to apply this match. On this occasion he meets with Blennerhasset.

"Who is Blennerhassett? A native of Ireland, a man of letters, who fled from the storms of his own country to find quiet in ours... on his arrival in America, he retired even from the population of the Atlantic states, and sought quiet and solitude in the bosom of our Western forests. But he carried with him taste and science and wealth; and lo, the desert smiled! Possessing himself of a beautiful island in the Ohio, he rears upon it a palace and decorates it with every romantic embellishment of fancy... Peace, tranquillity and innocence shed their mingled delights around him... In the midst of all this peace, this innocent simplicity and this tranquillity, this feast of the mind, this pure banquet of the heart, the destroyer comes; he comes to change this paradise into a hell... A stranger presents himself. Introduced to their civilities by the high rank which he has lately held in this country, he soon finds his way to their hearts, by the dignity and elegance of his demeanor, the light and beauty of his conversation and the seductive and fascinating power of his address. The conquest was not difficult. Innocence is ever simple and credulous. Conscious of no design itself, it suspects none in others. It wears no guard before its breast. Every door and portal and avenue of the heart is thrown open, and all who choose it enter. Such was the state of Eden when the serpent entered its bowers. The prisoner, in a more engaging form, winding himself into the open and unpracticed heart of the unfortunate Blennerhassett, found but little difficulty in changing the native character of that heart and the objects of its affection. By degrees, he infuses into it the poison of his own ambition. He breathes into it the fire of his own courage; a daring and desperate thirst for glory; and ardor panting for great enterprises, for all the storm and bustle and hurricane of life. In a short time the whole man is changed, and every object of his former delight is relinquished. No more he enjoys the tranquil scene; it has become flat and insipid to his taste. His books are abandoned... His ear no longer drinks the rich melody of music. It longs for the trumpet's clangor and the cannon's roar... Greater objects have taken possession of his soul. His imagination has been dazzled by visions of diadems, of stars and garters and titles of nobility... Yet this unfortunate man, thus deluded from his interest and his happiness, thus seduced from the paths of innocence and peace, thus confounded in the toils that were deliberately spread for him, and overwhelmed by the mastering spirit and genius of another – this man, thus ruined and undone and made to play a subordinate part in this grand drama of guilt and treason, this man is to be called the principal offender, while *he*, by whom he was thus plunged in misery, is comparatively innocent, a mere accessory! Is this reason? Is it law? Is it humanity? Sir, neither the human heart nor the human understanding will bear a perversion so monstrous and absurd! So shocking to the soul! So revolting to reason! Let Aaron Burr then not shrink from the high destination which he has courted, and having already ruined Blennerhassett in fortune, character and happiness forever, let him not attempt to finish the tragedy by thrusting that ill-fated man between himself and punishment.

"Upon the whole, sir, reason declares Aaron Burr the principal in this crime and confirms herein the sentence of the law; and the gentleman, in saying that his offense is a derivative and accessorial nature, begs the question and draws his conclusions from what, instead of being conceded, is denied. It is clear from what has been said, that Burr did not derive his guilt from the men on the island, but imparted his own guilt to them; that is not an accessory but a principal; and therefore, that there is nothing in the objection which demands a record of their conviction before we shall go on with our proof against him."[7]

It should be noted that, although Wirt's fame was based on his eloquence in what proved to be a losing cause, he also did a most workmanlike job in dismantling the defense. "The Blennerhassett passage in the Burr Trial speech, with its figure of Burr as the serpent in Eden, is remembered because it is romantic American rhetoric at its most characteristic. Actually Wirt followed closely the reasoning of his opponents and replied point for point or advanced new points of his own, but this the general public then as now has forgotten," observed Richard Beale Davis in *Intellectual Life in Jefferson's Virginia, 1790-1830*.[8]

Wirt also exhibited his quick courtroom wit in his exchange with a young militia fifer named Gates, who had been on duty against the conspirators and had witnessed the seizure of some boats on the Ohio River:

Wirt: "As far as I understand you, you were called on to attack the boats?"

Gates: "Yes."

Wirt: "And you were called on to carry a musket?"

Gates: "Yes."

Wirt: "And you were unwilling to do it?"

Gates: "Yes."

Wirt: "That is, you were willing to whistle and not to fight?"

Gates: "Yes."[9]

Despite Wirt's best efforts to charm and persuade the jury, the prosecution's case collapsed under an opinion handed down on key motions by Chief Justice Marshall on August 31. That opinion, one of Marshall's longest, taking three hours to read, was that: "Those only who perform a part, and who are leagued in the conspiracy, are declared to be traitors." To do so, it was necessary that the traitor "perform a part which will furnish the overt act, and they must be leagued in conspiracy." In any case, the overt act of war must be proved, and sworn by two witnesses. And the assemblage which levies war must be a "warlike assemblage, carrying the appearance of force, and in a situation to practice hostility." Marshall also attacked the idea of trying Burr before his alleged co-conspirators: "If those who perpetrated the fact be not traitors, he who advised the fact cannot be a traitor." Thus limited in what it could consider, the jury did not take long in rendering a verdict: "We of the jury say that Aaron Burr is not proved to be guilty under this indictment by any evidence submitted to us. We therefore find him not guilty."[10]

Deflated, Hay dropped the treason prosecution of the other defendants, very small potatoes compared to Burr, and reported the jury's finding to the President. Jefferson was irate, urging Hay to preserve all of the evidence that Marshall refused to allow the jury to hear. Wirt wrote to his friend Dabney Carr on September 1, 1807: "Sick as I have been for several days, and harassed by the progress of Burr's affair, I have but a minute to answer your favor by the last mail... Marshall has stepped in between Burr and death. He has pronounced an opinion that our evidence is all irrelevant, Burr not having been *present* at the island with the assemblage, and the act itself not amounting to levying war. The jury thus sent out without evidence, have this day returned a verdict, in substance, of not guilty."[11]

The misdemeanor trial of Burr took another 15 days, with some 50 witnesses testifying. But the results were much the same, the prosecution being unable, within the parameters established by Marshall, to prove to the jury's satisfaction that Burr planned anything hostile to Spain except in the event of war between the two countries. Hay then tried to have Burr and his associates tried for treason in the District of Ohio. Marshall ruled on October 20 that the affair had been aimed solely against Mexico.[12]

The trial was damaging to the reputations of both Burr and Jefferson, and to a lesser extent Marshall, who wore his Federalist sympathies on the sleeve of his judicial robes. But Wirt's performance in a losing cause was adjudged so spectacular that he emerged a winner in the eyes of many. His speech to the jury contrasting Burr and Blennerhassett has been preserved as one of the era's finest example of courtroom oratory and was recited by generations of school children as a classic example of American oratorical excellence.[13] In his early years at the bar, Wirt had been called by Marshall and his cronies a "Whip Syllabub Genius," a backhanded compliment to the young lawyer's ability to stir up a frothy courtroom concoction out of lackluster evidentiary ingredients. But, by the time of the Burr trial, Wirt was well on his way to becoming a sound legal scholar as well as a stellar performer in the courts. [14.]

Chapter 10

The Political Arena Beckons

As important as the Burr trial was to Wirt's career, the lawyer found himself distracted by another threat to the nation's security. On June 22, 1807, the *Leopard*, a 50-gun British frigate, fired on the American frigate *Chesapeake,* killing one sailor and wounding several, and causing Capt. Barron to strike his flag and allow the British to impress four of his crew, who were said to be British subjects. The act fired the patriotic imagination of a whole generation of American men who had been too young to fight in the Revolution and thirsted for revenge. William Wirt was one of them. Although the emotions unleashed by the *Chesapeake's* surrender would simmer until erupting in the War of 1812, Wirt immediately prepared to take up arms in the summer of 1807 (the Burr trial notwithstanding). As early as July 2, Wirt wrote to Dabney Carr to enlist him in a scheme to raise a legion to fight the British. "We are on tiptoe for war. I write this in the antechamber, where we are waiting the final resolve of the Council, on detaching a portion of us to support our brethren at Norfolk. On July 19, Wirt again wrote Carr about the impending campaign: "If so, what will you do with yourself? Not sit idly at home, I presume. For my part, I am resolved. I shall yield back my wife to her father... to which the old gentleman has agreed, and I shall march." It was not as humble privates that Wirt envisioned himself and Carr, but as gallant leaders of men. "We begin with four colonels – who are nominated, and of whom you are proposed to be one,'" he wrote. The others were Wirt, A. Stuart, a member of the Richmond Council, and John Clarke, the Superintendent of the Manufactory of Arms, whom Wirt termed, "one of the first geniuses and best men of the state."[1]

Things began to unravel a bit from that point on, however. On July 28, Wirt had to inform Carr, who was, of course, Jefferson's nephew, that he had been demoted in rank: "In the event of Nelson's being taken in as colonel, you will be my first major; and, when I take the command of the brigade, you will, of course, take the head of my regiment, which is the first regiment." At the end, Wirt added that the "Governor has written to the President in support of our letter." On August 12, Wirt wrote Carr to opine that, "the war cannot, in the nature of things, be a long one. A single campaign will probably give us Canada and Nova Scotia." By Sept. 1, the day after the Burr verdict, Wirt observed, "we have certainly been deceived, if not in the virtue, at least in the understanding of our countrymen. In spite of the repeated efforts which have been made to explain the motives and object of our association, and its non-interference with militia dignitaries, they still misapprehend it, or affect to misapprehend it." A week later, Wirt alluded to a rival legion proposed by Randolph and confessed, "I begin to apprehend that there will be no war. The blood of our countrymen has been washed from the decks of the Chesapeake, and we have never learned how to bear malice." By Sept. 14, Wirt's army appeared doomed: "As to the Legion, it has given me a new view of human nature and of my countrymen; and has, I confess, filled my heart with the most melancholy presages for their future destiny..." he wrote Carr. "So, 'we bring up the lee-way with a wet sail,' as poor Frank Walker used to say." On Sept. 22, Wirt noted, "It depends, I suspect, on Great Britain, whether the Legion will be ever filled up."[2] As it transpired, war with England was put on the back burner for five years.

President Jefferson may have misinterpreted Wirt's willingness to abandon his law practice and don military uniform as job dissatisfaction and an unfulfilled desire for public service. On January 10, 1808, Jefferson wrote Wirt and attempted to prod him into a run for Congress: "I suspected, from your desire to go into the army, that you disliked your profession, notwithstanding that your prospects in it were inferior to none in the state. Still, I know that no profession is open to stronger antipathies than that of the law. The object of this letter, then, is to propose to you to come into Congress. That is the great commanding theatre of this nation, and the threshold to whatever department of office a man is qualified to enter. With your reputation, talents and correct views, used with the necessary prudence, you will, at once, be placed at the head of the republican body in the House of Representatives... If you come in at the next election, you will begin your course with a new administration... you will become the Colossus of the republican government of your country. I will not say that public life is the line for making a fortune; but it furnishes a decent and honorable support, and places one's children on good grounds for public favor... Had General Washington left children, what would have been denied to them? Perhaps, I ought to apologize for the frankness of this communication. It proceeds from an ardent zeal to see this government (the idol of my soul) continue in good hands, and from a sincere desire to see you whatever you wish to be. To this apology I shall only add my friendly salutations and assurances of sincere esteem and respect. – *Th. Jefferson.*"[3]

Though flattered, Wirt respectfully declined. "I cannot better deserve your good opinion than by answering your proposition in the same spirit of frankness in which it was made," he wrote the President on January 14: "My desire to go into the army proceeded from no dislike of my profession. It arose from the impulse which electrified the continent... I have a wife and children entirely unprovided for. They subsist on the running profits of my practice. The instant this ceases they must either starve, or be thrown on the charity of their relations. The situation of our amiable and beloved countryman who has just returned from a foreign shore, to meet the most perplexing embarrassments, of a private nature, at home, is an awful lesson on the subject of devoting one's self to his country before he shall have secured an independent retreat for old age," Wirt wrote, in a pointed reference to the financial problems of their mutual friend, James Monroe.[4]

"I might add that were my fortune other than it is, there is not in life a course on which I would enter with more spirit and ardor than that to which you invite me. The government is most dear to my affections... And after your retirement, the pure and enlightened man to whom we look, as your successor, (James Madison), will, in my opinion, have no equal on the theatre of public life. Yet notwithstanding this, I am sure that you will approve my motive in adhering to the practice of law."[5] Interestingly enough, neither Jefferson nor Wirt discussed the possibility that Wirt might make a bid for a congressional seat and fail to be elected. Although Wirt declined the President's invitation to run, he did not abandon the political arena altogether. There was in Virginia in 1808, a determined movement, headed by John Randolph of Roanoke, to deprive Secretary of State Madison of the opportunity to succeed Jefferson in the White House. At that time, the Republicans selected their presidential candidate through a caucus of party members in the House and Senate, rather than by convention. That caucus had nominated Madison, but Randolph and his cronies rejected him because of alleged complicity in the "Yazoo land settlement" in Georgia, Madison's co-authorship of "The Federalist" with Jay and Hamilton, and a contention that Madison suffered from a "wont *(sic)* of energy" of character. Randolph and his friends rejected the caucus' decision and proposed Monroe as a more acceptable compromise. Wirt took up pen and defended Madison and the caucus in three letters addressed "to the Protestors," and signed, "One of the People," which were published in the Richmond *Enquirer:*

"One of the people of the United States, to whom you have lately addressed yourself through the medium of the press, returns you his acknowledgments through the same channel, and as one of your constituents, he expects to be heard by you in his turn," Wirt wrote. "...instead of a protest breathing the elevated spirit of conscious truth and virtue, telling us of wrongs which we have suffered, *and proving them too,* we find ourselves insulted by an electioneering squib – weak and inconsistent in its charges – shuffling and prevaricating in its argument – poor, entangled and crippled in its composition... "You arraign the late caucus at Washington; but have not you yourselves, or at least the most distinguished among you, been members of caucuses on the very same occasion? "Were you not members of a caucus for this very purpose in the presidential election of 1800? You cannot deny it; you dare not deny it... No shuffling in the ranks, gentlemen. A caucus is right or wrong on principle... Yes, it is not Mr. Madison only, it is the administration which offends you. It is their united effulgence which produces all this agitation and screaming among the birds of night. They long for the day-fall, which better suits the dimness of their sight; for the season of darkness, when the peculiar conformation of their organs may give them an advantage, and their fierce and predatory spirit may have full scope for indulgence and satiety... And did you suppose that it would be in the power of such men as you are, to shake the gratitude and attachment of the people to such a man as Mr. Madison? ... he is one of those men with whom, if a person were to quarrel, he would be at a loss how to abuse..."[6]

Wirt dealt logically with the three major objections cited by Randolph and his friends in the same way he would have handled the prosecution's arguments in a courtroom. As to Madison's alleged "wont of energy," Wirt replied, "How has Mr. Madison shewn it? Was it standing abreast with the van of our revolutionary patriots, and braving the horrors of a seven years' war, for liberty – while you were shuddering at the sound of the storm and clinging closer with terror to your mothers' breasts? Was it, on the Declaration of our Independence... or will you find it in the manner in which he watched the first movements of the Federal Constitution; in the boldness with which he resisted, even in a Washington, what he deemed infractions of its spirit; in the independence, ability and vigor with which, in spite of declining health, he maintained this conflict during eight years? ...if energy consist, as you seem to think it does, in saying rude things – in bravado and bluster – in pouring a muddy torrent of coarse invective, as destitute of argument, as unwarranted by provocation, you will find great evidence of want of energy in his speeches. But if true energy be evinced, as we think it is, by the calm and dignified, yet steady, zealous and persevering pursuit of an object, his whole conduct during that period is honorably marked with energy."[7]

Always a student of oratory, Wirt compared the Congressional speeches of the opposition with those of Madison, concluding: "What a contrast! It is the noisy and short-lived babbling of a brook after a rain, compared with the majestic course of the Potomac. Yet you have the vanity and hardihood to ask for the proof of his talents... You defeat your own purpose, gentlemen; you wish to destroy Mr. Madison; but you force us to recall his services and to reflect how immaculate must be that life, against which malice itself can bring no better charges."[8]

Wirt's enthusiastic support of Madison put him in something of an embarrassing position because of his close ties to Monroe. Wirt had, in fact, been contacted by some of Monroe's supporters and asked to serve on a committee to boost his candidacy. Wirt declined. He wrote Monroe on February 8 to explain his action: "I was called on to act as one of the standing committee to promote your electoral ticket. I declined it; stating that although personally more warmly attached to you than to Mr. Madison – for I knew you much better – and although I thought it would make very little difference to the happiness of the people of the United States which of you was President, yet, for political considerations, I preferred Mr. Madison." Wirt went on to advise Monroe that it might be unwise for him to oppose Madison at the risk of being too closely associated, in the public's mind, with the Federalists, then in the minority in Congress.[9]

About the time that his spirited defense of Madison appeared in the local newspapers, Wirt received another call to seek elective office. He was drafted as a candidate for Richmond's seat in the House of Delegates against Col. Carrington, a venerable hero of the Revolution. Then as now,

Virginia state legislators could discharge their official duties without interrupting their professional careers – especially if they live in or close to Richmond. Wirt expressed his feelings over this unexpected honor in a letter to his wife from Williamsburg on April 11, 1808: "There is an election here today, which reminds me of that in Richmond. The total indifference with which I contemplate the Richmond election convinces me that political ambition is not one of my sins... It is no disparagement to any young man that a patriot so old, so long tried, so virtuous and so worthy in every point of view as Col. C is preferred to him. I regret extremely that, by being unintentionally and unexpectedly drawn into collision with him, I have been made to have the appearance of implying a doubt of his fitness, or of entertaining a vain opinion of my own; both which opinions I most sincerely disdain." Much to Wirt's professed surprise, he was elected.[10]

A reluctant candidate to begin with, Wirt's two-year exposure to Virginia's General Assembly cured him of any desire to continue in that capacity. Kennedy's biography is nearly silent on this chapter of Wirt's life. Wirt's single recorded accomplishment as a freshman delegate, according to Kennedy, was to serve on a special committee on international trade. Jefferson's trade embargo of 1807 failed to accomplish its goal of bringing Britain and France around to acknowledging America as an equal trade partner. Hardest hit by the dearth of foreign trade, the people of New England rebelled through federalist-controlled legislatures. Connecticut's lawmakers resolved that "whenever our national legislature is led to overleap the prescribed bounds of their constitutional powers," it then becomes the duty of state legislatures "to interpose their protecting shield between the right and liberty of the people and the assumed power of the General Government." Virginians were more loyal to Jefferson and less dependent on foreign trade. Wirt, who also served at the time on a civic committee to encourage the establishment of manufacturing in the South, was selected to write the Virginia resolutions on this topic, documents that vindicated Jefferson's administration and its trade embargoes. Despite this vote of confidence from Jefferson's home state, Congress rushed through a repeal of the embargo and Jefferson signed it on March 1, 1809, three days before leaving office.[11]

Delegate Wirt also led the unsuccessful fight against the *Execution Bill*, a "stay law" designed to suspend executions during the trade Embargo and three months after it was raised.

"Why must the inhabitants of our towns be made the victims of legislative proscription?" cried the representative of the City of Richmond, arguing that the bill was not the simple protection of the poor against the rich it purported to be. To illustrate his point, Wirt dazzled his fellow delegates with a mock dialogue between a poor carpenter, the creditor, and a wealthy farmer, the debtor. In addition, Wirt said, the bill violated that section of the U.S. Constitution which forbade the states to impair the obligations of a contract, and was therefore unconstitutional.[12]

Another losing cause Wirt supported in the General Assembly was that of his friend, Major John Clarke, who was dismissed as superintendent of the Virginia Manufactory of Arms. Clarke had a hot temper and bristled under criticism. And he may not have been entirely blameless for the inferior quality of weapons issuing from the state armory supervision. After his dismissal, however, Clarke would persuade Wirt to back him in a private venture that was no more successful, although it provided Clarke with many years of employment.[13]

Madison's first several years in the Presidency were no easier than Jefferson's last years. In an attempt to answer criticism of Madison's leadership, Wirt published several essays in the summer of 1909 under the title, "The Sentinel." Although the sentiments were similar to those expressed in "One of the People," Wirt changed his writing style in an attempt to confuse readers as to the identity of the author. So familiar was Wirt to the readers of the Republican press in those days, that he felt a *nom de plume* was insufficient camouflage. Unfortunately, so was his attempt at a new style. The public was not deceived. Somewhat chagrined at the notoriety achieved by the missiles he periodically fired at the opposition party, Wirt remarked to Carr, "I hope I shall be prudent some time or other, though I sometimes doubt whether my scribbling so much in the papers is an evidence of it."[14]

Chapter 11

The 'Old Bachelor' Essays

From 1808 to 1812, Wirt's life finally settled into a steady pattern. His law career grew, as did his family. He sampled elective office and satisfied himself that it was not his cup of tea – a conviction he would hold for more than two decades. This period of relative stability also afforded Wirt an opportunity to solidify his position as a writer and orator of more than average ability.

Wirt discussed his financial and philosophical unsuitability for a political career in a February 26, 1809 letter to Benjamin Edwards, the father of his boyhood schoolmate, Ninian, who took Wirt into his home at a crucial stage of adolescence: "You wish me to aspire to the Presidency of the United States... I make no such extravagant calculations of future greatness. If I can make my family independent and leave to my children the inheritance of a respectable name, my expectations, and, believe me, *my wishes*, will be fulfilled. For the office of Secretary of State, under Mr. Madison, I am just about as fit as I am to be the Pope of Rome – nor ought I, nor would I accept it, in my present circumstances. It would be a sacrifice to my wife and children on the altar of political ambition. I have no such ambition, and my not having it, is one among a thousand proofs that I am unfit for that kind of life; for nature, I believe, never yet gave the capacity without the inclination."[1]

Five months later, Wirt again wrote Edwards, confidently predicting that by the time he was 45, he would have purchased a farm on the James River and would divide his attentions between the law and the life of a country squire. "There I will have my books, and with my family spend three seasons of the year... Those months I shall devote to the improvement of my children, the amusement of my wife, and perhaps the endeavor to raise by my pen a monument to my name... You see, there is no noisy ambition in it... It is true, I love distinction, but I can only enjoy it in tranquillity and innocence. My soul sickens at the idea of political intrigue and faction: I would not choose to be the innocent victim of it, much less the criminal agent. Observe, I do not propose to be useless to society. My ambition will lie in opening, raising, refining and improving the understandings of my countrymen by means of light and cheap publications."[2]

In 1810, Wirt revived his project to write a biography of Patrick Henry. This was originally planned to be the first of a series of biographies on major figures of the Revolution. Although but a child at the time of the nation's birth, Wirt held great admiration for the founding fathers, regardless of their political affiliation. So great was this admiration, that he sometimes despaired that his generation and the next generation lacked the greatness necessary to carry on the noble experiment in democracy. "Alas! poor country! what is to become of it?" he wrote Edwards. "Can any man who looks upon the state of public virtue in this country, and then casts his eyes upon what is doing in Europe, believe that this confederated republic is to last for ever? Can he doubt that its probable dissolution is less than a century off? Think of Burr's conspiracy, within thirty-five years of the birth of the republic... think of the state of political parties and of the presses in this country... Will not the people get tired and heart-sick of this perpetual commotion and agitation, and long for a change, even for king Log, so that they may get rid of their demagogues, the storks, that destroy their peace and quiet... Look at the debates in Congress. Where is the coolness, the decorum, the cordial comparison of ideas for the public good, which you would look for in an assembly of patriots and freemen, such as was seen in the old Congress of 1776? Nothing of it is now to be seen. All is rancor, abuse, hostility and hatred, confusion and ruin."[3]

In retrospect, Patrick Henry seems a curious choice for Wirt's first, and as it would transpire, only fling at biography. As a former republican who turned to federalism late in life, Henry was a thorn in the side of Wirt's political mentor. Like Wirt, however, Henry rose from humble beginnings to become a prominent lawyer and a consummate orator. In this context, Wirt's choice makes a great deal of sense. Henry qualified for Wirt's attention in another respect. The Hanover County patriot was dead and had been so for a number of years. After the embarrassment caused by his sometimes too accurate assessments of Richmond's prominent lawyers in *The British Spy* series, Wirt vowed to never again write about living persons. Because so little was recorded about Henry's life and thoughts – and even his major speeches, Wirt's search for information on Henry led him to those who had witnessed

Henry's role in the American Revolution and the early days of the new nation. Although he methodically strove for a balance, seeking input from Henry's political allies and foes alike, he was frustrated by the limitations of the subject.[4]

On January 18, 1810, Wirt wrote Jefferson, seeking his counsel on this matter: "About four years ago, you were so good as to state that if the 'Life of Henry' was not destined to come out very speedily, you would endeavor to recollect what might be of service to it; and that, having run your course with him for more than twenty years, and witnessed the part he bore in every great question, you would be able to recall some interesting anecdotes. In truth, so great is the inconsistency of the statements which I have received of his life and character, and so recent and warm the prejudices of his friends and his adversaries, that I had almost brought my mind to lay aside the project as one too ticklish for faithful execution at the present time..." Alas, Wirt said, he became more convinced with each day he spent in the Virginia Legislature that the biography of such a celebrated man might help inspire a little discipline in the current political scene, "...although I know very many much better qualified to give this discipline than myself, I hear of no one who is disposed to do it... Mr. Henry seems to me a good text for a discourse on rhetoric, patriotism and morals. The work might be useful to young men who are just coming forward into life."[5]

Although publication of Wirt's biography of Henry would prove to be several years off, his literary pursuits spawned several other projects, not the least of which was the *Old Bachelor* series of essays. Wirt began a series of essays called *The Sylph*, in 1810, but quickly shelved this project when he and several friends became engaged in the *Old Bachelor* series, which resulted in 33 essays published in the Richmond *Enquirer* between 1811 and 1813. Wirt was the ringleader in this literary enterprise, and is generally credited with writing the bulk of the essays. But it also featured the talents of St. George Tucker, George Tucker, Dabney Carr, Frank Carr, Francis and Peachy Gilmer, Richard E. Parker (later U.S. Senator and Judge of the Virginia Supreme Court of Appeals), Major David Watson of Louisa, and Louis Hue Girardin, an exiled French scholar and farmer. Because pseudonyms were used by the contributors to this project, attribution remains uncertain. Kennedy thought Wirt wrote the bulk of the 33 essays, but modern scholars differ on this. Wirt certainly wrote the opening essays in the series. Wirt is also generally credited with numbers 17, 18, 19, the first part of 9; 13, 14, 20, part of 12, and all of 31 and 32. Kennedy suggests Girardin as the author of numbers 11 and 12 and part of 10. Watson wrote part of 5 and may have written all of 33, or collaborated with Wirt on the final essay. Carr wrote the letter from "Obadiah Squaretoes" in number 9. George Tucker contributed two letters to number 15.[6]

Wirt introduced the "Old Bachelor" to readers thusly: "Alas! it is too true; I can no longer hide the melancholy fact, even from myself: I am, indeed, an Old Bachelor... for my fate is not a voluntary one... but as in every case, the lady was both judge and party, I fared as it might have been; I lost my suit." [7] Number 14 of the "Old Bachelor" also smacks of Wirt's touch, especially in its description of the ego and ambition of politicians: "There is no opinion that such a one advances, or represents, no man that he ensnares or praises, no dissenting shake of the head, no expression of countenance, no step that he takes, either in conversation or conduct, but what 'touches some wheel or verges some goal,' connected with the great affair of self. What an immense chain of causes and consequences, link after link, will he forge and put together in order to grapple the remote prize and bring it within his reach!"[8]   Number 17 compares the founding fathers to the politicians who replaced them: "Look at the remains of our revolutionary worthies – these plain, honest sons of valor and virtue – and compare them with 'the silken, ducking observants' of the present day. Is there not as much difference between them as there was between the contemporaries of Fabricus and those of Pompey at Rome?" [9]

In a letter to Carr, dated December 24, 1810, Wirt related a conversation with Parker in which he outlined the basic premise of the *Old Bachelor* essays, "with which he (Parker) was delighted, and agreed to contribute, provided I would sit at the helm, to preserve the unity of course and character... I mentioned to him that you and Frank would contribute, and he is very anxious to know you both... we agreed, for the reasons which I believe I suggested to you – the too palpable fiction, want of community and character and interests, and *unmanageability* – that the Sylph would not do. So I have hit upon another, the Old Bachelor, of which you will see two numbers, by the same mail which carries this. I like the plan myself, much. It gives scope for all sorts of composition; and I think, the adopted children of the Old Bachelor, will enable us to interweave something of a dramatic interest with the work. I shall assign the young doctor to Frank, and the young lawyer to Parker. You and I will manage the Old Bachelor and the

Niece."[10] The pivotal figure in the series was Dr. Robert Cecil, the old bachelor. "Galen" was Dabney Carr's brother, Dr. Frank Carr. "Alfred" was Parker. George Tucker was "Vamper" and "Peter Schryphel."

The Old Bachelor essays extolled the virtue of an education rich in the classics, forensic eloquence, and the social graces. They also touched on the subjects of gambling, avarice and patriotism. The announced aim, reminiscent of Addison, was, "virtuously to instruct or innocently to amuse." Professor Richard B. Davis saw the same theme of regret over the decline of Virginia's glory in "The Old Bachelor" that ran through "Letters of the British Spy" and "Rainbow," not surprising because of Wirt's participation. But Davis found "Bachelor" less melancholy and more sentimental than the other two series. There was, Davis continued, "a more insistent urge that 'the body of the people' be awakened to the need for education if the state is to return to her national leadership. Thus 'Virginia in decline' is a major theme as it is in much of the verse and some of the fiction of the period. 'Illustrious men! Immortal patriots! Where are ye now and your successors...' They are gone, the essayist adds, because the youth no longer apply themselves to serious study – because they lack the 'sublime enthusiasm of the past. Therefore, despite its nostalgic tone, the book is addressed to the rising generation."[11]

A great deal of correspondence passed between Dabney Carr and Wirt between 1810 and 1812, much of it having to do with the "Old Bachelor," its public acceptance, and to whom people had attributed the authorship of each installment in the lively parlor discussions the essays ignited. It was great fun for Wirt, but in a letter to Carr, dated February, 15, 1811, Wirt confessed that his combined role of lawyer, family man, essayist and editor was already getting to him: "What you tell me of the increasing fame of the Old Bachelor, is calculated, in some degree, to dispel the lassitude that is beginning to creep upon me in relation to the old fellow. I very frankly confess to you (though I would not do it to everybody) that I am tired of the project, even before I have reached the principal subject, education. But besides this, our courts are now made perpetual, and the Old Bachelor is rather in the way of business. I do not mean, by this, that I have resolved to drop him altogether; but, that he will see the light much more rarely than theretofore." Wirt also hinted to Carr that his collaborators were even less prolific than he: "Frank is a dastardly fellow. I had thought him a Corinthian – a lad of metal – but I now discover that he is – no better than he should be. Parker has not given me a single line. I have no more time to write now; and all this being about the Old Bachelor, does not look much as if I was tired of it"[12]

The 33 "Old Bachelor" essays were printed in book form in 1814. A "third edition" was issued in 1818 in Baltimore. The essays are generally judged the best literary effort of Wirt and many of his associates. After the essays were published as a collection, Philadelphia critic Robert Walsh labeled *The Old Bachelor* superior to any earlier volume of American essays. He called Wirt, "the finest genius that has ventured forth among us in the walk of literature." Others came along, of course, but 20th century scholars concede that Wirt was a pioneer in Virginia literature and give high praise to these essays. Davis noted, "Naturally the essays are extremely uneven, from the ability of the various authors and the degree of care they bestowed upon them. The *Old Bachelor* remains nevertheless the high watermark of the familiar essay in the early nineteenth century in Virginia and in some respects in the whole nation."[13]

About this point in his life, Wirt also attempted to write a play, a comedy entitled, *The Path of Pleasure*. It was never performed. Wirt showed several acts to friends, earnestly seeking their opinion, while wondering openly if it would enhance, or destroy his carefully cultivated image. St. George Tucker thought enough of it to pen a prologue and epilogue for the script. Although an enthusiastic patron of the theater who listed many actors as his friends, Wirt was conscious of the attitude of many 18th Century Americans toward the acting profession. This and the notion that his work simply wasn't good enough were factors in his abandonment of the play. Another factor may have been the tragic fire in Richmond's New Brick Theatre on Dec. 26, 1811, in which 72 lives were lost during a production of Green's Virginia Company. The Greens' daughter, who perished in the fire was to have had the lead role in Wirt's play. Wirt was still working on the play as late as 1815. He asked Tucker and his visiting brother to read the play, which he had apparently renamed, and to pass it along to Dabney Carr in Winchester, referring to it as "child of my fever and hype, *The Haunted Pavilion*, alias the *Path of Pleasure*." [14] Although generally worshipful of Wirt, Kennedy observed that it was probably just as well that the play was never produced.[15] Wirt wrote no more plays, but remained an enthusiastic patron of the theater. Richmond's "The Theatre," which opened in 1819 in a handsome brick and stucco building, was financed by stockholders who received a perpetual pass for their investment.

Wirt was one of them. Throughout his adulthood, Wirt yearned for the life of a writer, preferably one of independent means. Financial concerns and a penchant for setting aside both vocation and avocation for an evening of lively conversation and frivolity kept him from devoting as much time to literary pursuits as he maintained was his wish. Despite the occasional misstep, Wirt's popularity as a literary figure and man of quick wit continued to rise, however. This was aided in part by widely repeated anecdotes, such as one which occurred when Wirt and Jock Warden, an elderly, but feisty Scotsman sat in a Richmond court observing John Wickham carve up the progressively more angry U.S. Attorney John Hay. At one point, Wickham announced, "The gentleman may take which ever horn he pleases," which prompted Warden to whisper, "Take care of him. He has Hay upon his horn." Not to be outdone by the Scotsman, Wirt quickly penned the following epigram:

> *Wickham was tossing Hay in court*
> *On a dilemma's horns for sport,*
> *Jock, rich in wit and Latin too,*
> *Cries, "Habet foenum in cornu."*[16]

Chapter 12

The Realities of War

War with the British, an event that Wirt and other young patriots were so eager to rush into after the *Leopard* affair in 1807, eventually tested the resolve of the American people in 1812. Although warned by John Quincy Adams, then minister to Russia, that it was a trap leading to war, Madison forbade trade with Great Britain on March 2, 1811, under the authority of Macon's Act. Madison insisted that "the national faith was pledged to France." The winter of 1811-12 was the worst experienced by the English since the Great Plague. Wheat prices rose to $4.50 a bushel and manufactured goods piled up on the docks with no markets. Factories closed and workers rioted. Although the trade embargo came close to bringing the British to their knees, the U.S. Congress jumped the gun and declared war on June 18, 1812. Four factors were cited: impressment of American seamen, violations of territorial waters, the Royal Navy's paper blockade of the East Coast and the infamous orders of council against neutral trade. (Ironically, Lord Castlereagh suspended the orders of council two days before Congress declared war.) Most of the early action took place on the Canadian border and among rival Indian tribes on the frontier. But the threat of war was soon felt in Virginia.[1]

Although Wirt eventually answered the call to arms, it was with far less relish than he exhibited in 1807. He also discovered that war often involves more tedium and drudgery than action and glory. To be fair, it must be noted that citizen-soldier Wirt was a far different person in 1812 than he was in 1807. During the earlier crisis, Wirt was just reestablishing his professional credentials in Richmond, his sixth place of residence in 15 years as a lawyer. In 1807 he was willing to leave his wife and two children with his father-in-law, a former Revolutionary War officer, and rush off into battle, envisioning a speedy victory. In 1812, Wirt was 39 years old and the father of six children. Col. Gamble was killed by a fall from his horse on April 12, 1810, so there was no longer a sympathetic father-in-law to care for his family as Wirt rode off to war. Wirt had served in the state Legislature with distinction, if not relish, for two years and had been considered a candidate for U.S. Attorney General in 1811 – that appointment going to William Pinkney, the vastly more experienced Maryland lawyer who had been one of Wirt's boyhood inspirations. When war finally came in 1812, Wirt was not only approaching his 40th birthday, but he was much further along in his lifelong quest to become a man of substance.[2]

As the crisis with Great Britain escalated, a mutual friend told President Madison that Wirt might be interested in a commission in the Army. This prompted Wirt to write the President, declining the appointment: "However strong the desire to enter the service of the country actively," the situation of his private affairs would not permit it.[2] But when ships of the British squadron sailed up the James River as high as City Point in June, 1813, Wirt heard "the violent ringing of the alarm bell," raised a corps of flying artillery and was prepared to fight on his home turf: "...the Governor and field officers were clamorous and importunate for a company of flying artillery; and I could not resist their importunities, without submitting myself to the censure of indifference at least. So I raised a company for the defense of the town and neighborhood – and a most splendid one it is, amounting to near a hundred picked by me," Wirt wrote his wife, who was spending the summer at Montevideo. In a letter from Montevideo, Wirt described the events of that summer to Dabney Carr, now Judge Carr: "You would know what I have been doing this summer? Why, reading newspapers, mustering in the militia, hearing alarm bells and alarm guns, and training a company of flying artillery, with whom, in imagination, I have already beaten and captured four or five different British detachments of two or three thousand each... My wife and children were out of town. They were here; but I was 'in the thick of the throng.' " Mrs. Wirt, it would seem, took a dim view of her husband's soldierly activities at that point. "My wife is in uncommon health, but down-hearted because of the flying artillery, which she considers a boyish freak, unfit for the father of six unprovided children," Wirt wrote.[4]

By the following summer, however, the government had clipped the wings of Wirt's flying artillery, and he was reduced to the role of a militia leader in a lonely outpost. In a letter of July 7, 1814, to John Taylor Lomax, a friend who lived on the Rappahannock River in Richmond County, Wirt noted, "The Legislature have dismantled my flying artillery, by prohibiting the Executive from supplying us with horses and other munitions of war, whereby they have driven me into the ranks of the militia again, and there I stand until the war comes to me."[5] The war did not have far to go. On August 24, 1813, the British easily captured Washington, D.C., and sacked the White House. The enemy fleet sailed down the Potomac into the Chesapeake Bay, its destination unknown. Wirt and his militia were dispatched to a camp at Warrenigh Church on the York River, where they would await an enemy that never came.

Wirt's many dispatches to his wife from Warrenigh provide interesting insights into the role of an inexperienced captain in charge of a rapidly disintegrating band of volunteers:

September 9, 1814 – "Your most seasonable supply, under convoy of our man Randal, came in last evening. The starving Israelites were not more gladdened by the arrival of quails and manna, than we were by the salutation of Randal. The fish would have been a superb treat, had there been such an article as a potato in this poverty-stricken land. And yet the parish, according to the old inscription, is called 'Bliss-Land' – The church was built in 1709.

"The British fleet are said to have descended the bay, or to be now doing so. There was a seventy-four at the mouth of the York River, day before yesterday. She weighed anchor, yesterday, and went up the bay..."

September 12 – "Your kindness and thoughtfulness has filled my camp with luxury. I fear we shall have no opportunity to become memorable for any thing but our good living – for I begin to believe that the enemy will not attempt Richmond... We are training twice a day, which doesn't well agree with our poor horses. We have a bad camping ground – on a flat which extends two miles to the river – the water is not good and the men are sickly..."

September 13 – "An express this morning tells us that five square-rigged vessels are at the mouth of the York River. It is conjectured that the British fleet is coming down the bay. Their object of course, is only guess..."

September 19 – "The struggle, I now believe, will be a short one. The invincibles of Wellington, are found to be vincible, and are melting away by repeated defeats. The strongest blows they have been striking have been aimed only at the power to dictate a peace. A few more such repulses as they met at Baltimore, will extinguish that lofty hope, and we shall have a peace on terms honorable to us... Our volunteers are becoming disorderly for want of an enemy to cope with. Quarrels, arrests, courts-martial, are beginning to abound. I have had several reprimands to pronounce at the head of my company, in compliance with the sentence of the courts.... One of my sergeants deserted this morning... I am perpetually interrupted by the complaints of my men. Yet I do well, and if they leave me men enough I shall be prepared for a fight in a few days."

September 26 – "Still at Warrenigh, and less probability of an enemy than ever. We are doing nothing but drilling, firing national salutes for recent victories, listening to the everlasting and growing discontents of the men, and trying their quarrels before courts-martial. I have endeavored to give satisfaction to my company, so far as I could compatibly with discipline. My success, I fear has been limited... Frank Gilmer, Jefferson Randolph, the Carrs, Upshur, and others have got tired of waiting for the British, and gone home. David Watson is the only good fellow who remains with us. He is a major, quartered at Abner Tyne's – messes with us – takes six pinches of snuff to my one... He is an excellent fellow, and has spouted almost all Shakespeare to us. You may remember him as a contributor to the Old Bachelor. He, my second captain, Lambert, and my second lieutenant, Dick, make admirable company for me."

September 28 – "The Blues at Montpelier are suffering much from sickness. Murphy, your brother John and his friend Blair are all down. The other companies are almost unofficered – the men are very sickly. I strongly suspect that if we are kept much longer hovering over these marshes, our soldiers will fall like the grass that now covers them. We hope to be ordered in a few days to Richmond.... If we should be ordered to Richmond, I have no idea that my company will be discharged. It will be kept there ready to march at a moment's warning."

Wirt's experiences with his militiamen in the marshes along the York River cured him of any lingering military ambitions. In another letter to his wife, he wrote: "I would not, with my present feelings and opinions, accept of any military commission the United States could confer... I will be a private citizen as long as I can see that, by being so, I shall be of use towards maintaining those who are dependent upon me; holding myself ever ready for my country's call in time of need... We shall soon see whether Lord Hill, who is expected on the coast with fourteen thousand men, will single out Virginia for his operations. My own impression is that he goes to the relief of Canada, which feels itself in danger from our recent successes there."[6]

Shortly after his militia unit was recalled to Richmond, Wirt went to Washington, D.C. on business and observed the nation's government picking up the pieces after the British attack. He wrote to his wife: "I am surrounded by a vast crowd of Legislators and gentlemen of the Turf assembled here for the races which are to commence to-morrow, The races! – amid the ruins and desolation of Washington... I went to look at the ruins of the President's house. The rooms which you saw so rightly furnished, exhibited nothing but unroofed naked walls, cracked, defaced and blackened with fire. I cannot tell you what I felt as I walked amongst them... From this mournful monument of American imbecility and improvidence, and of British atrocity, I went to the lobby of the House of Representatives – a miserable little narrow box, in which I was crowded and suffocated for about three hours, in order to see and hear the wise men of the nation. They are no great things. At five to Monroe's, and was cordially received by him... P— and I called on the President. He looks miserably shattered and wo-begone. In short, he looked heart-broken. His mind is full of the New England sedition. He introduced the subject and continued to press it – painful as it obviously was to him. I denied the probability, even the *possibility* that the yeomanry of the North could be induced to place themselves under the power and protection of England... He invited us to dine with him, but we declined, having planned an excursion to Bladensburg, and, perhaps, Baltimore... We then went to the War office. The Secretary kept me engaged in political conversation till four o'clock."[7]

Wirt further expounded upon the dim view he took of most of those who ran the government in that day in a letter to Dabney Carr, dated December 10, 1814: "Government, my friend, is but an uphill work at best; and not least perhaps, this elective government of ours, where the public good is the last thing thought of by the Legislator – his own re-election being the first. What a stormy life is this of the politician! What hardness of nerve, what firmness of mind and steadiness of purpose does it require to sit composedly at the helm, and ably at the same time! Give me a life of literary ease! This is, perhaps, an ignoble wish: but it is, still, mine. Let those who enjoy public life ride in the whirlwind! I covet not their honors – *although,* if necessary, I would not shrink from the duty."[8]

Chapter 13

Before the Supreme Court

Wirt planned to make his first appearance before the United States Supreme Court in February, 1815. He wrote to Dabney Carr on Dec. 10, 1814 of his expectations: "The preliminaries are not quite settled. Should they be so to my satisfaction, will you meet me there? I shall be opposed to the Attorney General, and, perhaps to Pinkney. 'The blood more stirs to rouse the lion than to hunt the hare.' I should like to meet them," Wirt wrote in anticipation.[1] Although he would spend several weeks in Washington that winter awaiting the high court's pleasure, his first case there was delayed until the following winter. The time was well-spent however, in visiting with the leaders of the national government.

A year later, Wirt's case went before the Supreme Court and he finally had "broken a lance with Pinkney," as he described it. Wirt's firsthand impressions of his boyhood idol were less than complimentary. This is evidenced in a letter to his former law student, Francis Gilmer, the youngest brother of Wirt's first wife: "He has nothing of the rapid and unerring analysis of Marshall – but he has, in lieu of it, a dogmatizing absoluteness of manner which passes with the million... At the bar he is despotic and cares little for his colleagues or adversaries as if they were men of wood. He has certainly much the advantage of any of them in forensic show. Give him time – and he requires not much – and he will deliver a speech which any man might be proud to claim. You will have good materials, very well put together, and clothed in a costume as magnificent as that of Louis XIV; but you will have a vast quantity of false fire..."[2]

The case that brought him to the Supreme Court was not worthy of a clash of legal titans, in Wirt's opinion. "It was a mere question between the representatives of a dead collector and a living one, as to the distribution of the penalty of an embargo bond... I was for the representatives of the deceased collector (who had performed most of the work before expiring) –

Pinkney for the living one. You perceive that his client was a mere harpy, who had no merits whatever to plead." Noting that many women were present in the court, Wirt said that Pinkney played up to them. "Closing his speech in this solemn tone, he took his seat, saying to me with a smile, 'that will do for the ladies...' He is certainly not of the olden school."[3]

In a letter to Carr, his old confidant, Wirt confessed that his own courtroom preparation also left something to be desired. Wirt said he spent his first night in Washington chatting with an old friend until 2 a.m. "Immediately after breakfast I retired to my room, borrowed the acts of Congress, on which my cause arose, when several of my warm-hearted friends rushed into my room and held me engaged 'till court hour. So it was again in the evening; and so, on Thursday morning. In this hopeless situation, I went to court to try the tug of war with the renowned Pinkney... To be sure, these considerations gave me a sort of desperate, ferocious, bandit-like resolution: but what is mere *brute* resolution with a totally denuded intellect? I gave, indeed, some hits which produced a visible and animating effect; but my courage sank, and I suppose my manner fell under the conscious imbecility of my argument. I was comforted, however, by finding that Pinkney mended the matter very little, if at all. Had the cause been to argue over again on the next day, I could have shivered him; for his discussion revived all my forgotten topics, and, as I lay in my bed on the following morning, arguments poured themselves out before me as from a cornucopia... I must somehow or other contrive to get another cause in that court, that I may shew them I can do better."[4]

The Supreme Court would become a familiar arena much sooner than Wirt imagined at this stage in his career. About the time Wirt was wrapping up his business in Washington, George Hay resigned his post as U.S. Attorney for the Richmond District. Abel P. Upshur, a young attorney who had studied law under Wirt's direction, was mentioned as a candidate for the post. Wirt wrote a letter of reference to President Madison, urging him to consider Upshur. After praising his former student, Wirt said, "It is proper for me to state that he is a Federalist," but, "he justified the late war with Great Britain, and he was among the volunteers who marched to York Town to meet the enemy... I am entirely certain that no differences of political sentiment would ever swerve him from his duty, or abate, in the smallest degree, the zeal proper for its discharge." While this letter illustrates Wirt's nonpartisan attitude and his willingness to go to bat for a friend, it did little to sway the President, who already had a more experienced man in mind. Wirt's letter to Madison was dated March 10th, 1916. Madison wrote a letter to Wirt on March 13th, asking him to take the job. Somewhat embarrassed by the turn of events, Wirt wrote back on March 23rd: "I beg you to believe me unaffectedly sincere in declaring that there is nothing in the office which excites any solicitude, on my part, to possess it; and that I feel myself much more highly honored by the terms in which you were so good as to make the inquiry, than I should by the possession of the office itself... I assure you, with the frankness which I hope our long acquaintance warrants, your bestowing it on any one of the many gentlemen of my profession in this State who are, at least, equally entitled to it, and stand, perhaps, in greater need of it, will not, in the smallest degree, mortify me nor diminish the respect and affection with which I am and ever have been your friend."[5]

The post of U.S. Attorney for the Richmond District was not considered a full-time job in the early 1800s. Like many government jobs at that time, it did not pay well. Office holders were expected to make a living in some other manner or be independently wealthy. Happily for Wirt, the official duties were closely related to his profession and no relocation was required. He wasted no time in accepting. In truth, the conspicuous nature of the post was no deterrent to a private law practice and probably enhanced it, much the same as it is today for "part-time" state legislators.

On September 1816, Wirt received another honor, one which James Madison may also have had a hand in. Wirt was awarded an honorary degree of Doctor of Laws from Princeton University, Madison's alma mater. To someone like Wirt, whose formal education was interrupted at such an early age, this honorary degree had to be a significant honor and suitable recognition of an already illustrious law career. Also in 1816, Wirt was showcased in Francis Walker Gilmer's *Sketches of American Orators.* [6]

Early in 1817, Wirt argued his second case before the U.S. Supreme Court. Wirt represented the captain of a captured privateer in a case that hinged on whether or not the ship and her cargo were neutral or hostile property. "As counsel for the captured privateer, I was bound to contend that they were British; my adversaries, on the contrary, (Gaston and Hopkinson, against whom I stood alone), insisted that they were Russian," Wirt wrote Judge Carr. "...this issue of fact was to be decided by the analysis and synthesis of about five hundred dry, deranged ship documents, which were to be read and commented on. You perceive the utter impossibility of clothing such a subject either with ornament or interest; and when you are further told, that there was not one principle of dubious law involved in the case, you will as readily see that there was no opportunity for the display of any cogency of argument."[7]

Despite this handicap, Wirt was pleased with his performance, writing Carr, "I have been to Washington, and I made a speech, sir, in the Supreme Court *four hours and a half long!* Does this not alarm you? And will you not be still more alarmed when you are told that the court-room was thronged — fifteen or twenty ladies, many members of Congress, and, what is worse than all, the venerable Correa, whom I heartily wished in Portugal." Wirt assured Carr that he had other upcoming cases that would be better tests of his abilities: "... the one is a batture case, in which I have been employed against Livingston, by a family in New Orleans; another, a case from Virginia, in which I have been retained by the Literary Fund Society, on a question of the right of an alien to take the benefit of a devise of lands directed to be sold and the proceeds remitted to Scotland. The latter case will shew *[sic]* Wickham and myself in opposition; and though I shall probably lose the cause, I will give him a heat for the glory. You cannot conceive... what a rejuvenescence this change of theatre and of audience gives to a man's emulation. It makes me feel young again, and touches nerves that have been asleep ever since 1807 (the Burr trial).[8]

"Could I have supposed when you and I were treading the hog-paths through the wilds of Fluvanna, and trying to make our way at the bar of that miserable court, that a day would ever come when I could dare to hold up my head in the Supreme Court of the United States, and take by the beard the first champions of the nations! Who shall tell me after this that there is no God; no benignant disposer of events whose pleasure it is to raise the weak and lowly and down-trodden, by his own sovereign and irresistible *fiat?* No, sir, the prosperous events of my life have flowed from no prudence or worth of my own; but I feel at this moment, most gratefully feel, that they have been kindly forced upon me by an overwhelming providence."[9]

Chapter 14

A 'Life of Patrick Henry'

Wirt's "biography" of Henry, *Sketches of the Life and Character of Patrick Henry,* finally appeared in print in the autumn of 1817 and was an instant success, despite a mixed reaction from the critics and those who had known Henry. Many newspapers and the reading public were glowing in praise. Less generous were some of Henry's contemporaries and the northern literary reviews. The primary criticism was that Wirt tended to magnify Henry's virtues and accomplishments and minimize many of Henry's failings – a fault of many biographers. Wirt was also criticized for fleshing out Henry's speeches and placing too much weight on the events leading up to the American Revolution and Henry's influence on these events – faults that grew out of the scarcity of written records Henry left behind and Wirt's stated objective of providing the youth of succeeding generations with a hero they could emulate. Henry's life and his major speeches were pieced together from the memories of those who witnessed them. They were primarily Virginians who witnessed the American Revolution from that vantage point and had no reason to speak ill of their dead comrade, which accounts for some of the bias perceived by the Adamses and others who saw the Revolution develop in Boston.[1]

Somewhat favorable reviews appeared in the *North American Review, Analectic Magazine, American Monthly Magazine* and the *Virginia Evangelical and Literary Magazine.* The book was in its 25th edition by 1871, and, even though many 20th century scholars fault it for containing more fiction than fact, they make liberal use of Wirt's "Henry" as a source. Many of those finding fault with "Henry" as legitimate biography nevertheless hailed it as a remarkable literary achievement. Jefferson who was a major source for information about Henry and who read several proofs – was cautious in his praise, saying, "those who take up the book will find they cannot lay it down, and this will be the best criticism." John Taylor of Caroline called Wirt's book "a splendid novel." John Randolph, never one of Wirt's biggest fans, declared it "a wretched piece of fustian."[2]

John Adams was one of the severest critics, while conceding, "Your Sketches of the Life of Mr. Henry have given me a rich entertainment. I will not compare them to the Sybil conducting Eneas to the regions below to see the ghosts of departed sages and heroes; but to an angel conveying me to the abodes of the blessed on high, to converse with the spirits of just men made perfect... If I could go back to the age of thirty-five, I would endeavor to become your rival – not in elegance of composition, but in a simple narration of facts, supported by records, histories and testimonies of irrefragable [sic] authority." Adams went on to explain that Wirt's "Henry" robbed the patriots of Boston of much of their luster, contending that the resistance to British rule dated back to 1760, when "James Otis electrified the town of Boston, the Province of Massachussetts Bay and the whole continent, more than Patrick Henry ever did in the whole course of his life. If we must have panegyric and hyperbole, I must say that, if Mr. Henry was Demosthenes and R.H. Lee Cicero, Mr. Otis was Isaiah and Ezekiel united."[3]

In a letter to Adams, dated January 12, 1818, Wirt admitted that he may have been too lavish in crediting the Virginian for such a major role in the Revolution, "but if I have done so, I can affirm with the most solemn truth that I have not sinned intentionally... It was far from my inclination, I beg you to be assured, as it was from the scope and object of my work, to institute an invidious comparison between the States of Massachussetts and Virginia in the Revolutionary contest. I had been led by the histories of the times to consider them as twin sisters in this race of glory, and as running fairly abreast through the whole course of it... the single object which I had in view was to discharge my portion of that debt of national gratitude, which I thought justly due to a great benefactor of his country."[4]

Wirt was aware, several years before "Henry" was published, that his project was rife with pitfalls. In 1815, he wrote the following to his friend Carr: "Now for Patrick Henry. I have delved on to my one hundred and seventh page; up-hill all the way, and heavy work, I promise you; and a heavy and unleavened lump I fear me it will be, work it as I may. I can tell you, sir, that it is much the most oppressive literary enterprise that ever I embarked in, and I begin to apprehend that I shall never debark from it without 'rattling ropes and rending sails.' I write in a storm, and a worse tempest, I fear, will follow its publication..."

Among the problems Wirt said he had encountered was the difficulty in pinning down exact dates of Henry's key speeches from the collected memories of those he had contacted. "And in addition to the dates, I have the facts themselves to collect. I thought I had them all ready cut and dry, and sat down with all my statements of correspondents spread out before me... thinking that I had nothing else to do but, as Lingo says, 'to saddle Pegasus, and ride up Parnassus.' ...I found, at every turn of Henry's life, that I had to stop and let fly a volley of letters over the State, in all directions, to collect dates and explanations, and try to reconcile contradictions." Wirt also confessed to difficulty reconciling his free-swinging essayist style to a more factual task. "...I find that it is entirely a new business to me, and I am proportionately awkward at it... the style of narrative, fettered by a scrupulous regard to real facts, is to me the most difficult in the world. It is like attempting to run, tied up in a bag. My pen wants perpetually to career and frolic it away... The incidents of Mr. Henry's life are extremely monotonous. It is all speaking, speaking, speaking. 'Tis true he could speak – Gods! how he *could* talk! But there is no acting 'the while.' From the bar to the legislature, and from the legislature to the bar, his peregrinations resembled, a good deal, those of someone, I forget whom – perhaps some of our friend Tristram's characters, 'from the kitchen to the parlor, and from the parlor to the kitchen.' I have dug around it and applied all the plaister [sic] of Paris that I could command; but the fig-tree is still barren... 'Then surely you mean to give it up?' On the contrary, I assure you, sir: I have stept in so deep, that I am determined, like Macbeth, to go on."5

Judge St. George Tucker influenced the final product through advice and opinions on rough drafts. Along with Jefferson, Tucker was one of Wirt's primary sources on Henry's unrecorded speeches. Henry's famous 1775 "Give me Liberty or Give me Death" address, as recorded by Wirt, came mainly from Judge Tucker's memory. It was a reconstruction in an era when there were no court reporters, tape recorders or VCRs. Wirt never intended that it be taken as a verbatim account. Modern scholars dispute its accuracy. Prof. Davis concluded, "at any rate, the three Virginians Henry, Tucker, and Wirt produced one of the stirring and most dramatic forensic passages of American history, a passage which has done much to make both the speaker and his surroundings a grand element of the American myth."[6]

After a thorough study on the authenticity of Wirt's version of Henry's "Liberty or Death" speech, David Arnold McCants concluded that Wirt did a better job than many of his critics believed. "Wirt's method of reporting the speeches conforms to scholarly requirements and constitutes an important basis for confidence in the authenticity of his report of Henry's most celebrated address, the speech in 1775 Virginia Convention." Henry's family seemed more than satisfied with Wirt's account and were undoubtedly relieved that Wirt portrayed Henry as hero, rather than the scoundrel some of his political opponents thought him to be. Henry's grandson, William Wirt Henry (his name implies the ultimate compliment to Henry's biographer) believed Wirt's version of "Liberty or Death" came mainly from an eleven-page letter from St. George Tucker. McCants also noted that Tucker was twenty-three when he heard Henry's speech, which placed him in a better position to remember it with accuracy than witnesses who were in their 70s and 80s when Wirt tested their memories. And, although Tucker may have been more impressionable at twenty-three, he also didn't even like Henry, so he had no reason to embellish the speech. [7]

St. George Tucker also steered Wirt away from orthodox biography. On April 4, 1813, Tucker wrote, "American biography, at least since the conclusion of the peace of 1783, is a subject which promises as little entertainment as any other in the literary world... How would you be able to give an entertainment to your readers, in the Life of Patrick Henry, without the aid of some of his speeches in the General Assembly, or Congress, in Convention, or in the federal Court? What interest could be excited by his marrying a Miss ——, and afterward a Miss D——; and that somebody, whom I will not condescend to name, married one of his daughters, &c., &c., &c. No human being would feel the smallest interest in such a recital... The same may be said of Lee, Pendleton and Wythe; and the same may be said of every other man of *real merit*, in Virginia. They have all glided down the current of life so smoothly, (except as public men,) that nobody ever thought of noticing how they lived, or what they did; for, to live and act *like gentlemen*, was a thing once so common in Virginia, that nobody thought of noticing it."[8]

Jefferson also influenced Wirt's final product, although with the great many friends who contributed information, suggestions and editing input, Wirt could not follow everyone's recommendations. Jefferson indicated that Wirt's "Henry" was "a little too poetical" for his taste and suggested Wirt "prune" some of the "excrescences." It was advice the author chose to ignore, in part because he was under pressure from an impatient printer who had already announced the book, and because others had praised the manuscript. Jefferson, who was not enamored with Henry in the first place, also objected to Wirt's flowery comparisons of Henry to a mountain stream, a river, a cataract and finally to the ocean beating against the shore. "As at present advised, however," Wirt told his friend Carr, "I believe I shall hazard it, though not without fear and trembling, I confess." Jefferson later said Wirt was guilty of embellishing Henry's education in his effort to portray a man youngsters could emulate. Wirt wrote that Henry "read Plutarch every year." To this, Jefferson commented drolly, "I doubt if he ever read a volume of it in his life."[9]

The hero Wirt created for the new generation of Virginians, to which he dedicated his book, was undoubtedly larger than life. When Henry rose to persuade his fellow Virginians that rebellion against Great Britain was the only course open to them, Wirt wrote, "His was a spirit fitted to raise the whirlwind, as well as to ride in and direct it. His was that comprehensive view, that unerring prescience, that perfect command over the actions of men, which qualified him not merely to guide, but almost to create the destinies of nations."[10]

Wirt said Henry challenged his reluctant listeners: "Ask yourselves how this generous reception of our petition comports with those warlike preparations which cover our waters and darken our land. Are fleets and armies necessary to a work of love and reconciliation? Have we shown ourselves so unwilling to be reconciled, that force must be called on to win back our love? Let us not deceive ourselves, sir. These are the implements of war and subjugation – the last arguments to which kings resort... They are sent over to bind and rivet upon us those chains which the British ministry have been so long forging. And what have we oppose to them? Shall we try argument? Sir, we have been trying that for the last ten years... What terms shall we find, which have not been already exhausted? Let us not, I beseech you sir, deceive ourselves longer. Sir, we have done everything that could be done, to avert the storm which is now coming on... *There is no longer any room for hope...* I repeat it, sir, we must fight! An appeal to arms and to the God of hosts, is all that is left us! ...There is no retreat, but in submission and slavery! Our chains are forged. Their clanking may be heard on the plains of Boston! The war is inevitable – and let it come!! I repeat it, sir, let it come!!!

"It is vain, sir, to extenuate the matter. Gentlemen may cry, peace, peace – but there is no peace. The war is actually begun! The next gale that sweeps down from the north will bring to our ears the clash of resounding arms! Our brethren are already in the field! Why stand we here idle? What is it that gentlemen wish? What would they have? Is life so dear, or peace so sweet, as to be purchased at the price of chains and slavery? Forbid it, Almighty God – I know not what course others may take; but as for me,' cried he, with both arms extended aloft, his brows knit, every feature marked with resolute purpose of his soul, and his voice swelled to its boldest note of exclamation – 'give me liberty, or give me death!'

"He took his seat," Wirt wrote. "No murmur of applause was heard. The effect was too deep. After the trance of a moment, several members started from their seats. The cry, 'to arms!' seemed to quiver on every lip and gleam from every eye!"[11]

William Robert Taylor, a Harvard professor writing in the *William and Mary Quarterly*, in the 1930s put Wirt's *Henry* in perspective, saying Wirt sought approval from all, seeking a sort of literary "acquittal." Wirt this time "almost ended up with a hung jury... Although the book was much criticized at the time it was published and is now conceded very little authority in what it says of Henry's life and times, it initiated a kind of historical writing which was almost wholly new. Wirt's critics could not even find a word to describe it; they thought the book unique even when, like Adams and Jefferson, they were unreceptive... 'Panegyric,'" the word most frequently used, "hardly fits the bill... Wirt wrote of Revolutionary times in Virginia as a golden age, an age of heroes... He made no effort to conceal his belief that such men and such times would never again return."[12]

How much of what we know as Henry's speeches were Henry, how much of them Wirt and how much of them St. George Tucker and others will always be debated. The descriptions of Henry's oratorical splendor are certainly vintage Wirt. When Henry spoke, according to Wirt, "There was no rant – no rhapsody – no labor of the understanding – no straining of the voice – no confusion of the utterance. His countenance was erect – his eye steady – his action, noble – his enunciation, clear and firm – his mind poised on its centre – his views of his subject comprehensive and great." Henry's genius, "was unbroken, and too full of fire to bear the curb of composition. He delighted to swim the flood, to breast the torrent, and to scale the mountain... his genius was left at large to revel in all the wildness and boldness of nature; that it enabled him to infuse more successfully, his own intrepid spirit into the measures of the revolution." Henry's eloquence, Wirt said, "poured from inexhaustible fountains, and assumed every variety of hue and form and motion... Sometimes it was the limpid rivulet sparkling down the mountain's side, and winding its silver course between margins of moss – then gradually swelling to a bolder stream, it roared in the headlong cataract, and spread its rainbows to the sun – now, it flowed on in tranquil majesty, like a river of the west, reflecting from its polished surface, forest, and cliff, and sky – anon, it was the angry ocean, chafed by the tempest, hanging its billows, with defining clamors, among the crackling shrouds, or hurling them in sublime defiance at the storm that frowned above." [13]

Wirt's "Henry" was not a comprehensive biography capable of standing the test of time. Indeed, Wirt made no such claim. But it accomplished its original goal of providing Americans of succeeding generations with some insight into a man who was instrumental in creating the new nation. It also recorded for posterity remembrances of Henry that may have been lost had Wirt not taken the initiative. As Wirt feared, his "Henry" was the target of taunts not only from literary critics but from those who did not like the subject of the biography. A memorable one stated succinctly:

> HENRY'S eloquence and that of Wirt
> The roaring torrent, and the puffing squirt! [14]

Yet, today, many of the same scholars who condemn Wirt's work also quote freely from it. Professor Robert appropriately likened Wirt's versions of Henry's speeches to "a 'Williamsburg restoration,' authentic foundations and a superstructure built on the spirit of the times. ...one may safely conclude that the key phrases are authentic." [15]

Chapter 15

Attorney General of the U.S.

Wagilliam Wirt's name frequently came up when the political kingmakers of the day sought a qualified and popular figure for a particular office. In 1813, when it was rumored that Sen. Giles was thinking of resigning his seat, Wirt was contacted to see if he would accept appointment. When Giles did resign in 1815, Wirt was again contacted. Both times he took his name out of consideration. When Senator Richard Brent died in office in January, 1815, Wirt's friends in the state Legislature nominated him for the post without his knowledge. His close friend, Gov. Barbour, received the appointment. Kennedy surmised that had Wirt been offered the appointment he would have refused, especially since it would have come at the expense of an old friend. Despite – or perhaps because of – his disdain for elective public office and the poor opinion he held about many politicians, Wirt was often seen as a reluctant but draftable candidate.[1]

In the fall of 1817, shortly after the publication of Wirt's biography of Henry, Richard Rush resigned as United States Attorney General to accept an appointment as Ambassador to Great Britain. President Monroe asked Wirt to take the job and he accepted on Nov. 13. The appointment was confirmed by the Senate on Dec. 15. In January, 1818, Wirt reported to Washington, after first consulting with his wife, since the new job required him to establish residency in the nation's capital. (The residency requirement, when it was instituted in 1814, may have prompted Pinkney to resign, so lucrative was his Baltimore law practice.) The Attorney General was allowed to continue a private law practice, however, and this provision met Wirt's concern about providing for his family while serving the public.[2]

On January 18, 1818, Wirt expressed his feelings about his appointment in a letter to William Pope: "I have been long convinced that there is not enough iron in my composition for a public character: I mean for a politician aiming for glory... Nor would I have accepted any other office under the government, even the highest; for any other would have been utterly

incompatible with what I deem my first duty – which is to
provide for my household. 'He that provideth not for his
household is,' pronounced, you know, to be 'worse than an
infidel.' Nor am I vain and foolish enough to aim at anything
higher. I am already higher than I had any reason to expect...
The salary, you know, is very low, only three thousand
dollars. There is talk of raising it. I wish it may not end in talk.
As to the other business in the Supreme Court, I have as yet
only eight or ten causes; but I have a prospect of more in the
course of the approaching court and the fees are good."[3]

To another old friend, Judge Carr, he wrote on January 21,
1818: "We are here, sir, established in our own house, for the
which I have this day paid twelve thousand dollars... The office I
find is no *sinecure*. I have been up till midnight, at work,
every night, and still have my hands full. Much of this is
properly not my duty... My single motive for accepting the office
was the calculation of being able to pursue my profession on a
more advantageous ground – i.e. more money for less work.
Ulterior objects never were within my view and never can be.
Many of my friends took follies of this sort, but you will believe
me sincere when I assure you there is not a speck of them
within the horizon of *my* hopes or wishes... An honorable and
easy old age is all I desire. How far beyond what I had any
reason to count on in my youth... The Supreme Court is
approaching. It will half kill you to hear that it will find me
unprepared; but I shall contrive ways and means to keep my
professional head, at least, above water. As to any great figure
I cannot promise it, in the bustle in which I am now engaged. As
yet, I have not paid, or even returned one single visit: forty-three
visits in debt this day..."[4]

Despite his characteristic disclaimers, Wirt threw himself
into the task ahead with great vigor. He quickly discovered
that previous occupants of the office had wandered far from the
job description, as defined by Congress, and that little had been
done to record and preserve past decisions by the Attorney
General. In the 12 years and two administrations under which
he held the post, Wirt reorganized the office on a professional
basis and set policies that exist today. Because of his willingness
to be on call and the strong personal and political ties he had
with Monroe, Wirt was the first Attorney General to become a
full-fledged member of the Cabinet. The duties of the office, as
prescribed by law, were, "to prosecute and conduct all suits in
the Supreme Court, in which the United States are concerned,
and to give advice and opinions upon questions of law

when required by the President, or when requested by the heads of any of the departments, touching matters that may concern their departments." The Attorney General's opinions were "not merely persuasive upon the judgment of other officers, but, so far as the construction of the law is concerned, regarded as binding; and, if error be committed, the responsibility is, in a great degree, taken from them and cast upon him – a responsibility by no means light to a sensitive and well organized mind," Samuel L. Southard noted in a memorial tribute to Wirt delivered in the House of Representatives on March 18, 1834.[5]

One of Wirt's first major cases as Attorney General was the prosecution of three men accused of an armed mail robbery in Harford County, Maryland, on March 11, 1818. Wirt conducted three separate trials on May 9-12, seeking the death penalty in all three cases. A simple robbery would have carried a ten-year maximum sentence, but Congress had enacted a law calling for the death penalty in cases where the mail robber was a second offender, or where the robber imperiled the life of the mail carrier. With his soft-spot for youth, Wirt offered to enter a *nole prosequi* on the capital counts against 20-year-old Lewis Hare, if he pleaded guilty to simple robbery. However, Hare, like his co-conspirators, Joseph Thompson Hare and John Alexander, opted for trial by jury.

In the first case, with Joseph Hare as defendant, mail carrier David Boyer testified that three white men wearing blackface stopped him on the Baltimore-Philadelphia turnpike and assaulted him with "pistols and dirks," robbing him of "bank bills, letters and packets." Wirt explained to the jurors that the law made a distinction between a robbery and an armed robbery that placed the mail-carrier's life in jeopardy, "by the use of dangerous weapons... The weapon used is a pistol; a weapon fabricated for the very purpose of danger to life; it is used because it is dangerous," Wirt said. "What mercy would there be to the virtuous part of society, in letting loose upon them, men (if such monsters deserve the name of men) of this description?" Wirt asked the jury. After a two-hour deliberation, the jury found Hare guilty as charged.

In the *United States v. John Alexander,* which took place two days later, Wirt told the jurors to consider themselves on one hand "the trustees of the lives and property of the community and the life of the prisoner on the other." Wirt said the mail was "public property... it goes to relieve the wretched; to bear comfort to the afflicted; to aid the merchant in prosecuting his commercial concerns..." After a 90-minute deliberation, the jury found Alexander guilty. On May 12, after similar testimony, the jury also found Lewis Hare guilty on all counts. But Wirt appealed to President Monroe to pardon the 20-year-old defendant on two of the charges, leaving only a ten-year prison sentence. John Alexander and Joseph Hare were executed. [6]

As early as March 27, 1818, Wirt called the attention of Congress to several defects he saw in the past operation of the Attorney General's office: "...my first inquiry was for the books containing the acts of advice and opinions of my predecessors: I was told there were none such. I asked for the letter-books, containing their official correspondence: the answer was that there were no such books. I asked for the documents belonging to the office; presuming that, at least, the statements of cases which had been submitted for the opinion of the law-officer had been filed, and that I should find, endorsed on them, some note of their advice in each case; but my inquiries resulted in the discovery that there was not to be found, in connection with this office, any trace of a pen indicating, in the slightest manner, any one act of advice or opinion which had been given by any one of my predecessors, from the first foundation of the federal government to the moment of my inquiry."[7]

Wirt added that the previous occupants of the office had been "in constant danger of being involved themselves, and involving the departments which depended on their counsel, in perpetual collisions and inconsistencies." Wirt did not blame his predecessors, he said, because no one had thought to pass a law making that the policy of the government. He also criticized the fact that the office had not been furnished with copies of the laws of individual states and that everyone, from congressmen down to customs collectors, routinely called on the Attorney General for opinions that he, by law, was not permitted to give. He opined that this widespread misuse of the Attorney General's time could have something to do with the rapid turnover in the office. In April, 1818, Congress grudgingly acquiesced to some of Wirt's demands. Space for an official Attorney General's office was provided in the Treasury Building and a clerk was authorized with an annual salary of $1,000. In May, 1819, Congress approved a $500 contingency fund for the office. The Treasury also provided a writing desk and chair for the clerk, a map stand, two book presses, six extra chairs, two wash stands, a small table and a water pitcher and glasses. After three decades of operation, the federal government finally provided the Attorney General with a permanent office. Congress never approved Wirt's request for an adequate law library while he was in office.[8]

Through his persistence and longevity, Wirt was able to institute sweeping changes in the operation of his office. Based on his interpretation of constitutional guidelines, he denied opinions to private persons and even many government officials. But he found it difficult to deny opinions to the same congressmen he was asking for salary increases and an office budget. Wirt's belief that the Attorney General's opinions should be preserved was carried out from that point on. Kennedy noted that when the 26th Congress authorized the printing of the collected opinions of the Attorney Generals, more than 500 of the 1500 pages in the volume were devoted to Wirt's opinions. "They all," said Southard, "relate to matters of importance in the construction of the laws; many of them to the most difficult and interesting subjects of municipal and constitutional law, as well as the law of nations, which occurred during three presidential terms. They will prevent much uncertainty in that office hereafter, afford one of the best collections of materials for writing the legal and constitutional history of our country, and remain a proud moment of his industry, learning and talents."[9]

Wirt immediately took to the hustle and bustle of Washington and cast a contemplative glance toward expanding his law practice not only in the nation's capital, but into his native state of Maryland. He described Washington and nearby areas of Maryland to his friend William Pope, shortly after assuming the duties of Attorney General. "A beautiful place it is, I promise you, in the spring and summer. I shall have leisure to ride with you to all of the surrounding heights which overlook Georgetown, Washington, Alexandria, and the seats on the Potomac as low down as Mt. Vernon; and I will carry you to Bladensburg, the place of my nativity; shew you the house in which I was born... And if you come next summer, you will probably see a seventy-four gun ship launched, which you will find in the stocks, next month, at our navy yard. 'What a great nation we are,' and how much greater we will be, if we hold on as we have begun!"[10]

His position as Attorney General was the ticket Wirt used to gain entrance to the Maryland bar, although he had no residency there. In the spring of 1818, Wirt represented the federal government in the prosecution of those accused of robbing a mail stagecoach on the road between Baltimore and Philadelphia. The stage driver was killed during the robbery.

Thanks at least in part to Wirt's abilities, the robbers were tried, found guilty, and sentenced to death. Wirt was exempted from the stringent regulations of the Maryland bar on the grounds that his official duty entitled him to that privilege in cases involving the government. Over the next twelve years, Wirt enlarged this loophole and built up a lucrative law practice in his native state, while still a resident of the District of Columbia. After his first successful outing in the Maryland courts, he wrote Francis Gilmer: "Whether I shall make anything of it remains to be seen. There is a mighty harvest there, and their reapers are many; but their sickles are Lilliputian. There is but one Brobdignag scythe in the field – and that is Pinkney's."[11]

Although he was regarded as one of the nation's best court-room lawyers upon his appointment as Attorney General at age 46, Wirt still had a few personal benchmarks to measure up to. One of them was William Pinkney, who was eight years older, and in whose footsteps Wirt seemed to follow. Pinkney was one of the young lawyers whom Wirt had watched in court as a teenager. Trained in both law and medicine, Pinkney had served as a state delegate and senator, U.S. Congressman, commissioner to London under the Jay treaty, joint minister to England with Monroe (1806-1807) and sole minister (1807-1811). Pinkney was U.S. Attorney General from 1811 to 1814, minister to Russia and special envoy to Naples (1811-1814). He was elected to the U.S. Senate in 1818. Wirt and Pinkney would clash many times in the Maryland Courts and the U.S. Supreme Court from 1818 until the latter's death in 1822.

It was a contest Wirt thirsted for. "Pinkney is really a fine creature in his profession... has a fertile and noble mind... A debate with Pinkney is exercise and health," Wirt wrote to Pope. "I should like to see you on his weather-bow. I verily believe you could laugh him out of court; but as for me, I am obliged to see him out in hard blows. With all his fame, I have encountered men who hit harder. I find much pleasure in meeting him. His reputation is so high that there is no disparagement in being foiled by him, and great glory in even dividing the palm. To foil him in a fair fight, and in the face of the United States – *on his own theatre,* too – would be a crown so imperishable, that I feel a kind of youthful pleasure in preparing for the combat." Their courtroom rivalry became so intense near the end of 1818 that a duel was averted only through the intercession of mutual friends.[12]

Although he made the Attorney General's office more professional in many respects, Wirt's dependence on outside cases for a livelihood raised a few eyebrows. Many of his predecessors had the wherewithal to subsidize their lifestyle and official duties with personal fortunes. Wirt did not. He was continually under fire from political opponents in the House and Senate for what they perceived as a conflict of interest, although none of this talk evolved into any successful action. In true lawyerly fashion, Wirt had no problem with representing a private client in court and, at a later date, dealing with the same person or company as Attorney General, either as advocate or adversary. Wirt's efforts to limit the services his office offered while enthusiastically wooing private law clients continued to be a taxing exercise, however.

Chapter 16

Wirt and the Marshall Court

Wirt's first year as Attorney General was a relatively quiet one, enabling him to establish his household in the nation's capital, begin the reorganization of the office and build up the cushion of private law practice that would allow him to continue as Attorney General longer than anyone who had held that post. But in 1819, Wirt rocketed to national attention for his participation in two landmark cases before the Supreme Court, *McCulloch v. Maryland* (the Bank of U.S. case) and *Dartmouth College v. Woodward* ("the Dartmouth College Case."). Both cases involved Wirt with Daniel Webster, the first as associate, the second as opponent. In *McCulloch v. Maryland,* Wirt, Webster, and their associate Pinkney triumphed. In the Dartmouth College Case, it was Webster and his associate Joseph Hopkinson (who wrote the song, "Hail Columbia") triumphing on behalf of the plaintiff over Wirt and John Holmes.[1] Despite the credentials of the lawyers involved, both cases are remembered as examples of the "Marshall Court's" decisions on state's rights. So powerful was Chief Justice John Marshall's influence over the Supreme Court during his of service, (1801-1835), that he dissented only eight times. Of the court's 1,106 opinions during this era, Marshall wrote 519 of them.[2]

John Calhoun introduced the bill that chartered the second Bank of the United States in 1817. It passed and began operations. The bank's major client was the U.S. government, which was also a major stockholder. The Bank of the U.S. differed from the Bank of England in that it established branches in major cities. Although necessary for the government to operate efficiently, this feature handicapped smaller banks operating under state charters. In retaliation, the Maryland Legislature levied a heavy tax on the notes issued by what it contended was "a foreign corporation." The bank refused to pay. Maryland's position was upheld by its own court of appeals and the case went to the Supreme Court. Three major issues were at stake: (1) Are the states separately sovereign, or are the people of the U.S. collectively sovereign? (2) Was the Congressional Act chartering the bank constitutional? (3) If so, did the state reserve the right to tax its operation?

On the first point, Maryland's lawyers argued state sovereignty, basing this on Jefferson's Kentucky Resolutions of 1798. On the second item, Maryland based its case on Jefferson's opinion on the bill chartering the first Bank of the United States, arguing the fact that there was no federal bank from 1811 to 1817 proved that it was not necessary, and that all powers not expressly granted to the federal government are reserved by the states. Although it must have pained Wirt to argue against Jefferson's opinion on this case, he saw his duty as Attorney General and had no problem doing so. Wirt and Webster argued, with Marshall concurring, that the national government emanates from the people and that its powers are granted by them for their benefit. They cited Hamilton's opinion of the First Bank of U.S., that the powers of the federal government, while limited, are supreme within its sphere of action. As to the taxation question, it was argued that states have no power of taxation to retard, impede, burden or control the operation of the constitutional laws passed by Congress. The federal government's arguments and the Marshall court's opinions did not go down well in Maryland. "A deadly blow has been struck at the sovereignty of the states," a Baltimore newspaper declared. [3] But the Supreme Court's ruling was consistent with Marshall's long-standing policy of sanctioning the doctrine of centralization of powers at the expense of the states.

The Dartmouth College case involved a second Marshall principal: that the constitution protects private property rights from attacks by the states. This case resulted from an action by the New Hampshire Legislature to abolish the college's pre-revolutionary charter and place it under state control. Webster represented his alma mater, the plaintiffs in error, with characteristic eloquence. The court's ruling protected privately endowed colleges and schools from political interference and encouraged endowments for education and charity. Wirt's arguments for the defense were not fully recorded, but were well received, despite the court's ruling. Webster wrote to Wirt after this trial, praising his opponent's performance: "It is the universal opinion in this quarter, amongst all who have inquired or heard about the cause, that

that argument was a full, able and most eloquent exposition of the rights of the defendant. I will add that, in my opinion, no future discussion of the questions involved in the cause, either at the bar or on the bench, will bring forth, on the part of the defendant, any important idea which was not argued, expanded and pressed in the argument alluded to."[4]

Piracy and the slave trade prompted many of the cases before the Supreme Court in the early 1800s. An 1819 law directed the President to maintain a naval patrol off the African coast and authorized $100,000 to be used to return to Africa blacks illegally brought into the United States. It also attached the death penalty to slave trading. Secretary of the Treasury William Crawford championed the American Colonization Society and wanted the $100,000 used to create an American colony in Africa populated by illegal slaves. Wirt argued unsuccessfully that the law did not allow this, suggesting that Congress be consulted. Wirt, later won over to the cause by Crawford and Monroe, okayed the use of these funds by the Society in creating Liberia, the capital of which is Monrovia. A flaw in the scheme was the inability of the United States to break up the lucrative slave trade. Wirt pointed out that local customs collectors were charged with preventing slave ships from being outfitted in American ports, but they were liable for damages if they seized a ship on insufficient evidence. Wirt stood by his basic belief that slavery was an existing condition and must be dealt with as such. In the *Antelope* case, Wirt argued against the return of blacks to Spanish and Portuguese owners, saying, "Slavery was introduced among us during our colonial state, against the solemn remonstrances of our legislative assemblies. Free Americans did not introduce it... The Revolution which made us an independent nation, found slavery existing among us. It is a calamity entailed upon us by the commercial policy of the parent country." Justice, humanity, the law of nations and the laws of the United States pronounced these Africans free men, Wirt argued. His argument was hailed by a Boston reporter as "worthy of all praise," but condemned by Gov. George Troup of Georgia.[5]

Historians have observed that the story of Wirt's twelve years in the office of Attorney General is the story of the Marshall Court. Indeed, Marshall dominated the Supreme Court at which Wirt spent much of those years practicing, representing either the federal government or private clients. One observer went so far to say that Wirt arrived in Washington a Jeffersonian Republican and left a Marshall

Federalist.[6.] This is somewhat unfair to Wirt, however. In truth, prior to becoming Attorney General, he already held Marshall in high regard as a legal mind, freely recommending to the many young lawyers he advised that they look up to Marshall as someone worth emulating. As a dedicated lawyer, Wirt was visibly frustrated when the Chief Justice ruled against his clients' interests. On the other hand, his interests as Attorney General often were upheld by the Marshall Court. Prior to coming to Washington, Wirt had frequently expressed the fear that the nation was endangered by too strict an adherence to states' rights, and he would continue that theme. Wirt retained a cordial relationship with Marshall, often delivering letters between Marshall and his wife, who resided in Richmond during court terms.

Wirt was not alone in his concern for the survival of the nation. The economic panic of 1819 created a profound distrust of the federal government and the Bank of the U.S. in the western states when that institution refused to renew personal notes and mortgages, thus causing the collapse of many state banks. The Missouri Compromise of 1820 put the issue of slavery on the back burner for several decades, but added to concerns that the nation could not survive the constant threat of state and regional interests.

The issue of national sovereignty versus state's rights again came to a head in the Supreme Court in 1824, with the case of *Gibbons v. Ogden*. Known as the "New York Steamboat Case," the court's decision not only smashed a state-chartered monopoly, but mapped out the course Congress would follow for interstate commerce for more than a century. Wirt and Webster once again teamed up in this case, in opposition to a state granting exclusive rights to navigate its waters. Emmett, one of the attorneys for New York, argued that the state had granted such a monopoly to Fulton and Livingston on the basis that the genius and effort Robert Fulton put into the development of the wondrous steamboat should not go unrewarded. "And the happy and reflecting inhabitants of the States they (the waters of the Ohio and Mississippi Rivers) wash, may well ask themselves whether, next to the constitutions under which they live, there be a single blessing they enjoy from the art and labor of man, greater than what they have derived from the patronage of the State of New York to Robert Fulton?"

Had he left well enough alone, Emmett might not have supplied Wirt with a golden opportunity. But Emmett tried to gild the lily with a classical allusion, saying that "New York may raise her head, she may proudly raise her head, and cast her eyes over the whole civilized world... and justly arrogating to herself the labors of the man she cherished, and conscious of the value of her own good works, she may exultantly ask, *Quae regio in terris, nostri non plena laboris?*" Wirt relished the opportunity to question the relevance of Emmett's Latin quote: "Sir, it was not in the moment of triumph, nor with the feelings of triumph, that *Aeneas* uttered that exclamation. It was when... he was surveying the works of art with which the palace of Carthage was adorned, and his attention had been caught by a representation of the battles of Troy... the whole extent of his misfortunes, the loss and desolation of his friends, the fall of his beloved country rushed upon his recollection:

'Consitit, et lachymans, quis jam locus, inquit, Achate, Quae regio in terris, nostri non plena laboris?'

"Sir, *the* passage may hereafter have a closer application to the cause than my eloquent and classical friend intended," Wirt said. "For, if the state of things which has already commenced, is to go on; if the spirit of hostility which already exists in three of our States, is to catch by contagion and spread amongst the rest... what are we to expect? Civil wars, arising from far inferior causes, have desolated some of the fairest provinces of the earth. History is full of the afflicting narratives of such wars... It is a momentous decision which this Court is called on to make. Here are three states almost on the eve of war. It is the high province of this Court to interpose its benign and mediatorial influence... (and) harmonize the jarring elements in our system. But, sir, if you do not interpose your friendly hand, and extirpate the seeds of anarchy which New York has sown, you *will* have civil war... Your country will be shaken with civil strife. Your republican institutions will perish in the conflict... Then, sir, when New York shall look upon this scene of ruin... it will not be with her head held aloft, in the pride of conscious triumph, 'her rapt soul sitting in her eyes,' No, sir, no! Dejected with shame and confusion, drooping under the weight of her sorrow, with a voice suffocated with despair, well may she exclaim, '—quis jam locus — Quae regio in terris nostri non plena laboris?'" [7]

The Supreme Court took such action as Wirt and Webster sought. Marshall opined: "... the power over commerce with foreign nations and among the several states is vested in Congress as absolutely as it would be in a single government... The power therefore is not to be confined by state lines, but acts upon its subject matter whenever it is to be found."[8]

Wirt was one of the most active lawyers before the Supreme Court in the first third of the 19th century, arguing 174 cases in 14 years, an average of 12 cases per Supreme Court session. He won 96 of them and lost 68. (In ten cases the Court made no clear decision.) During his nearly 12 years as Attorney General, Wirt argued 138 cases before the Supreme Court. Only 39 were government cases, but Wirt won more than two-thirds of those. Although Wirt and Marshall may have had some philosophic differences, Wirt put his clients' interests first when he appeared in court. And in a majority of the cases Wirt tried before the Supreme Court, he and Marshall were in agreement.[9]

Chapter 17

Counsel to Presidents

In serving as Attorney General of the United States for nearly two full terms under James Monroe and for another full term under John Quincy Adams, William Wirt set a record for longevity in that office that still stands. The longest anyone held that post before Wirt was Charles Lee, who served at the pleasure of George Washington and John Adams for six years, from 1795 to 1801. Since Wirt, only Thomas W. Gregory (1914-1919), Homer Cummings (1933-1939), Herbert Brownell Jr., (1953-58) and Robert F. Kennedy (1961-65), have served more than four years. Given the pressures of the office, vagaries of politics and intensive scrutiny of the media today, it is doubtful if anyone will ever equal Wirt's longevity.[1]

Today, Wirt is not accorded the status of being among the nation's greatest attorney generals. But he has been called "the first great Attorney General."[2] He certainly was the first professional Attorney General. In the early days of the country, the Attorney Generals, operated out of their hip pockets, traveling from their homes to the nation's capital, only when summoned by the president or pressing business in the Supreme Court. It was not until 1814 that the Attorney General was required to reside in Washington, D.C. Although he continued to maintain a lucrative private law practice, as was the custom in that day, Wirt organized the office of the Attorney General in systematic fashion and fled the Capital only during the unhealthy summers and when cases drew him to distant cities.[3]

Wirt is also accorded the distinction of being the first Attorney General to participate actively in government decisions as a member of the President's Cabinet. His advice was sometimes ignored, and as events would prove, his advice was sometimes wrong. But in his Attorney General, Monroe found more than a lawyer. Wirt became a player in the nation's decision-making process.

An early opinion of Wirt's, one that gathered dust in manuscript form in the National Archives for over a century and a half, enjoyed a flurry of attention in the early 1970s, when President Nixon fought the subpoenas of federal prosecutors during the Watergate Investigation. On January 3, 1818, President Monroe was subpoenaed to give testimony in the naval court martial of Dr. William P.C. Barton, a surgeon at the Philadelphia Naval Hospital charged with conduct unbecoming an officer. On January 13, Wirt told Monroe, "A subpoena *ad testificandum* may I think, be properly awarded to the President of the U.S." But Wirt advised Monroe to duck the issue by giving the Judge Advocate a respectful answer, while pleading a conflict of government duties which would prevent him from appearing at a trial in Philadelphia. On the basic question of whether the president could be forced to appear in court against his will, Wirt said the federal courts had never expressed an opinion.[4]

Wirt's opinion had its roots in an incident more than a decade before in which he also played an active role. During the Burr trial, in which Wirt was co-prosecutor, Justice Marshall issued a subpoena on President Thomas Jefferson. Although he was incensed at Marshall's gall, Jefferson also used the excuse that pressing government business prevented him from appearing in Richmond and offered to give testimony by deposition. Burr never demanded a warrant under which Jefferson could have been arrested and brought to trial to testify, so the court never had a chance to rule on the propriety of this. In another trial in New York, the court was divided over the decision to issue an attachment compelling heads of executive branches to testify in trials.[5]

On the question of an attachment, Wirt advised Monroe and Adams to follow their own consciences on the question, "without resting on my opinion in a case which can scarcely be considered as exclusively within the province of the lawyer." But he went on to suggest that the issue could be circumvented by following Jefferson's method in the Burr case. According to the record of the court martial, Monroe took that advice in replying to the subpoena. He stated that he would not attend court, but offered depositions. By that time, the court martial had been concluded, with Dr. Barton receiving a reprimand. Although not a factor, Monroe's response was filed with the court papers.[6]

Although taking the easy way out by leaving the final decision up to Monroe, his friend and benefactor, Wirt was not insensitive to the potential repercussions of his response. Monroe's action, he noted, "may, by possibility, involve the executive in a collision with the judiciary," adding that the question was one "of great delicacy and importance." Wirt's opinion emerged from obscurity during the Watergate investigations, being cited by the U.S. Court of Appeals for the District of Columbia.[7]

In his advice to Monroe on the powers of the Presidency, Wirt subscribed to the strict Jeffersonian belief that Congress was the final arbiter on most executive decisions. As Commander in Chief of the armed forces, the President had "final appellate power" in courts martial. "But let us not claim this power for him, unless it has been communicated to him by some specific grant from Congress, the fountain of all law under the Constitution," Wirt added. The President had the power to control his subordinates in order to ensure the laws of the land were carried out effectively, Wirt argued. But the President was not personally responsible for enforcing these laws, and it was up to the courts, not the Chief Executive, to interpret the meaning of the laws, Wirt believed.[8]

Wirt's Jeffersonian background influenced many of his views on slavery. Although he abhorred the practice on moralistic grounds, he saw nothing wrong with owning slaves as long as it was legal to do so. Sometimes this led to seemingly contradictory reasoning. In an 1821 opinion, Wirt said that the President was under no compulsion to return to Great Britain a British crew from a ship seized by pirates and sailed into an American port, unless so instructed by Congress. But in 1822, he issued another opinion saying that the President was obligated to return a fugitive slave who had escaped from the Danish Island of St. Croix, noting that the power to restore the slave to his owner did not differ from the President's power to return foreign property. "The President is the executive officer of the laws of the country; these laws are not merely the constitution, statutes, and treaties of the United States, but those general laws of nations which govern the intercourse between the United States and foreign nations."[9] Adams was angered by Wirt's regard for slaves as property, writing in his diary, "The truth is, that between his Virginian aversion to constructive power, his Virginian devotion to States rights, and his Virginian autocracy against slaves, his two opinions form the most absurd jumble of self-contradictions that could be imagined. If the President has not the power to deliver up a pirate, he cannot possibly have the power to deliver up a slave."[10] Despite Adams' frustration, Wirt's opinions were soundly grounded on the existing laws and upheld by the courts of the day.

Wirt's opinions also expressed a reverence for the judicial system honed in a lifetime of practice before the courts. He often advised Monroe and Adams that they had the constitutional power to act, while cautioning them that it would be wise to refer most questions to the courts. Burke noted that Wirt gave two reasons for this, that such a policy would prompt the courts to rule on the matter as soon as possible, and that a conflict between the executive and judicial branches should be avoided, when at all possible. Wirt also declined to issue an opinion on many matters pending before the courts. In one case, Burke noted, Wirt reversed an opinion when the Virginia Court of Appeals took the opposite position. "The case is altered, and the opinion of the court of appeals must be our guide," Wirt said.[11]

Wirt's extensive private law practice caused him to miss many Cabinet meetings. John Quincy Adams noted in his diary that between 1821 and 1828, Wirt missed 57 cabinet meetings for reasons other than illness. Adams also observed of Wirt: "He has two faults which may have an influence in the affairs of this nation, an excessive leaning toward State supremacy and to popular humors." But Wirt's input was welcomed by Monroe, and, after some initial reservations, by Adams. In the early days of the Monroe Administration, Adams noted in his diary, "Wirt and Crowninshield will always be of the President's opinion." After he became president, apparently, Adams found such loyalty more desirable in a cabinet member. A non-believer in the political spoils system, Adams had no reservations about retaining Wirt as Attorney General.[12]

Monroe established a practice of calling in cabinet members for discussion of all national issues and administration policies. These meetings were run on a very informal basis, with Monroe summoning members by short, handwritten notes, as illustrated by the following examples:

J.M. will be glad to see Mr. Adams at 12 o'clock today, to meet the other heads of departments, on the subject of the war, with an Indian tribe, to the south.

Mr. Calhoun, Mr. Thompson and Mr. Wirt are here, in consequence of a suggestion that we would meet, on the subject of trade with British Colonies. Will you come over and intimate the same to Mr. Crawford? -- J.M.[13]

Monroe made an attempt to satisfy different sections of the country and widely divergent political views in assembling his Cabinet, which made for lively discussions. Secretary of War John C. Calhoun was a staunch defender of slavery. Secretary of State John Adams was vehemently anti-slavery. William H. Crawford, who stayed on as Secretary of the Treasury, harbored hopes of becoming president after Monroe. Westerner Henry Clay, who also had presidential aspirations and coveted the State Department, felt insulted when Monroe offered him the War Department, refusing to attend the inauguration. (Adams would offer Clay the position of Secretary of State in 1825.)

On more than one occasion, Wirt's talent as a writer was used by the Monroe Administration. When Gen. Andrew Jackson's unauthorized invasion of Florida put Monroe in a sticky diplomatic situation that had the potential for an international flare-up, Wirt ghost wrote an editorial for the *National Intelligencer* that laid out the administration's position.[14] The article stated that, "In attacking the posts of St. Mark and Pensacola, with the fort of Barancas, General Jackson, it is understood, acted on facts, which were, for the first time, brought to his knowledge, on the immediate theatre of war; facts, which, in his estimation, implicated the Spanish authorities in that quarter, as the instigators and auxiliaries of the war; and he took these measures on his own responsibility merely." Monroe's own letter to Jackson was similar to Wirt's editorial, although it was more critical of Jackson's unilateral action, noting, "In transcending the limit prescribed by those orders, you acted on your own responsibility."[15]

Wirt was involved in several stormy cabinet meetings during the debate over the Missouri Compromise of 1820. Monroe was under intense pressure from his supporters in the South to veto the bill which restricted slavery in the territories. Monroe's son-in-law, George Hay, wrote him from Richmond, saying, "The members have gone up to the caucus under the impression that you will put your veto on this infamous cabal and intrigue in all its forms and shapes; this I would certainly and promptly do... The whole affair is regarded as a base and hypocritical scheme to get power under the mask of humanity, and it excites the most unqualified indignation and resentment..." Monroe prepared a draft of a veto message, one he never used, in which he labeled the compromise unconstitutional. He then asked his cabinet members if Congress had the constitutional right to prohibit slavery in the territories. All members agreed that Congress had this power, but neither Wirt, nor Calhoun, nor Clay could find any express powers to that effect.[16]

Wirt's dissenting voice was noted during the deliberations over what was to became the Monroe Doctrine. Wirt opposed the commitment of American armed forces against the superior resources of the Holy Alliance of European powers. He persuaded Monroe to tone down some of the belligerent language Adams had written into his message to the Russian Minister, Baron de Tuyll. Wirt contended the country would not support the government in a war for the independence of South America, and insisted that Adams delete "a hornet of a paragraph" from the final document. Wirt asked if the administration was prepared to go to war without the approval of Congress. Monroe advised everyone to sleep on it and in the morning wrote Adams a note asking him to delete all of the paragraphs objected to in the cabinet meeting. Arguing that the European powers would not risk war over South America at that time, Adams again pressed for inclusion of the "hornet sting." Monroe appeared to give in, cleverly leaving the final decision to Adams, if he deemed the offending paragraph essential. Put on those terms, Adams deleted the forceful language. Monroe adopted the language contained in the message to Baron de Tuyll, presenting it, in its modified version, in his message to Congress in 1823. It has lived on as the *Monroe Doctrine*.[17]

Adams retained most of the members of Monroe's Cabinet when he ascended to the Presidency in 1825. After spending early autumn in New England, Adams returned to Washington ready to take on Congress and shape the country according to his vision. Among the improvements Adams sought were a department of the interior, a national university, sweeping changes to the patent office, a national observatory, a national naval academy and the sponsorship, on a national level, of research and geographic exploration, especially in the Pacific Ocean and northwest coast of the continent. Richard Rush, who replaced Adams as Secretary of State, agreed with the plan, but doubted it would find favor with the rest of the cabinet officers. Clay and Barbour found fault with various aspects of the plan. "It is excessively bold," Wirt observed. "There is not a line in it which I do not approve. But it would give strong hold to the party in Virginia who represent you as grasping for power... It is a noble, spirited thing, but I dread its effects on my popularity in Virginia. They will cry down as a partiality for monarchies your reference to the voyages of discovery and scientific researches." Adams toned down some of his proposals, presenting the balance to Congress on December 5, 1825. "Liberty is power," Adams told Congress. "The nation blessed with the largest portion of liberty must in proportion to its numbers be the most powerful nation on earth..."[18]

Monroe and Adams continued to value Wirt's counsel after their presidencies. In 1831, as Monroe lay near death in New York at the house of his son-in-law and long-time private secretary, Samuel Gouverneur, Andrew Jackson's supporters attempted to rewrite history concerning Jackson's invasion of Florida in 1818. John Rhea of Tennessee wrote Monroe, attempting to trap the failing ex-president into admitting that he had, through Rhea, authorized Jackson's invasion of Florida before the fact. Distraught, Gouverneur sent the letter to Wirt, asking advice on how to handle the situation, and expressing his fear that the unfounded charge could agitate Monroe to the point it might affect his worsening health. Wirt told Gouverneur that a formal statement from Monroe was necessary to set the record straight. On June 19, 1831, fifteen days before he died, Monroe signed a deposition refuting Rhea's claims. "It is utterly unfounded and untrue that I ever authorized John Rhea to write any letter whatever to General Jackson, authorizing or encouraging him to disobey, or deviate from the orders, which had been communicated to him from the Department of War," Monroe stated.[19]

Chapter 18

Wirt and Jefferson

In the beginning of their relationship, Thomas Jefferson viewed Wirt as a bright young man with great potential. He steered Dr. Gilmer's new son-in-law into intellectual pursuits and molded him into a Jeffersonian Republican. After the death of Gilmer and his daughter, Wirt's wife, Jefferson pulled strings in the state Legislature to secure him the position of Clerk of the House of Delegates. When Jefferson needed a good lawyer to represent his and Party interests, as demonstrated by the Callender defense and the Burr prosecution, Jefferson called upon Wirt. Jefferson encouraged Wirt to run for political office, assuring him that he would become a leading light in the Party. Although Jefferson was unsuccessful in interesting him in a political career, Wirt's reputation as an able courtroom lawyer continued to rise in the eyes of the sage of Monticello.

Jefferson first called on Wirt's legal skills in 1795, in the case of *Cobbs v. Jefferson*. Jefferson dutifully recorded in his account book on June 16, 1796: "Pd Mr Wirt 5.D. fee in Cobbs' suit against me." At that time, Wirt was newly wed to the daughter of Jefferson's family physician. Employing the young lawyer may have been an act of friendship, or perhaps parsimony, considering the modest fee.[1]

But Wirt continued to support Jefferson and Jefferson did the same for Wirt. After Jefferson left the Presidency, Wirt and others put on a lavish dinner in Jefferson's honor at Richmond's Eagle Tavern. Wirt's toast was to "Unity, Friendship and Love," the Richmond *Enquirer* reported. Several weeks after the dinner, William Clark, probably on Jefferson's suggestion, asked Wirt to edit the journals of the Lewis and Clark Expedition. It was a task Wirt declined.[2]

In later years, Jefferson tended to specify Wirt's services in sensitive cases, making it clear that he thought Wirt a very able courtroom lawyer. After his Presidency ended, Jefferson stated that he expected the legal assistance of Wirt and George Hay (Monroe's son-in-law), "in all cases where I am not named

merely pro forma."[3] When served the writ in the Batture Case
(*Livingston v. Jefferson*), the sage of Monticello was livid, fearing
that John Marshall's "twistifications of the law" might ruin him.
Jefferson insisted Wirt, Hay and Wirt's old Norfolk associate
Tazewell represent him. To keep Monroe on his good side,
Jefferson communicated with his defense team through Hay,
while confiding in Dabney Carr, "I hope Mr. Wirt, understands,
the thing right, & knows that he is the principal with me."
Marshall dismissed the Batture Case on a jurisdictional
question. Jefferson was not completely happy with this result,
but promptly paid his attorneys. Wirt said he was not
comfortable collecting a fee of $100 for defending a President,
but accepted the money on the assumption that the government
would compensate Jefferson.[4]

Although Jefferson was openly disappointed with Wirt's
biography of Patrick Henry, Jefferson collaborated unstintingly
in the effort. Some of his disappointment in Wirt the author may
be attributed to the fact that Wirt ignored a number of
Jefferson's suggestions. Despite this minor setback in their
relationship, Jefferson retained great faith in Wirt's abilities as
a lawyer and undoubtedly exercised some influence in Madison's
choice of Wirt as U.S. Attorney for the Richmond District and
Monroe's selection of Wirt as Attorney General.

When Jefferson sought a professor of law for his new
University of Virginia in Charlottesville, he selected Wirt. Seven
of the eight chairs had been filled when the University opened in
1825. The Board of Visitors wanted Wirt so badly, in fact, they
were willing to circumvent Jefferson's intention that the
University operate without a chief executive. (Jefferson stuck to
his principles and had to be overruled by the board on this point,
however.) The Board of Visitors, which consisted of James
Madison, Joseph C. Cabell, John H. Cocks and Chapman
Johnson, instructed Jefferson to offer Wirt the twin
inducements.[5]

On April 6, 1826, Jefferson wrote the Attorney General:

*I have the pleasure to inform you that, by an unanimous vote
of the Rectors and Visitors of the University of Virginia, you have
been appointed Professor of the School of Law in that Institution.
To no one, I can assure you, is that appointment more gratifying
than to myself; and I may further say with truth and for your
satisfaction, that your name was amongst the first which
occurred to some of us at the epoch of the original nomination,
was the subject of consultation, and would have been that,
probably, of first approbation, but from the absolute despair of*

your relinquishing for this, the higher station you occupy. Some suggestions, however, having lately reached the Board that this might, possibly, be less desperate than was apprehended, they have, with a view to strengthen inducements to your acceptance, created an office of President of the University, with an annual salary of fifteen hundred dollars, and appointed you to that office also... Permit me to add the assurance of my great esteem and respect. – Thomas Jefferson[6]

The resolutions accompanying Jefferson's letter noted that the inducement of the presidency of the new institution was reserved for Wirt only:

Resolved, That William Wirt, at present Attorney General of the United States, be appointed President of the University and Professor of Law; and that if he decline the appointment, the resolution establishing the office of President be null and void.[7]

Had Wirt seen fit to accept the offer and return to a more slowly paced life in the foothills of the Blue Ridge mountains, he might have achieved his ambition to ease into a graceful retirement as a man of letters. But concern for the future of his wife and children was an overriding factor, and Wirt opted for another eight years of stress fighting battles in the state and federal courts and before the Supreme Court:

I beg you to be assured that I had no agency, direct nor indirect, in giving this trouble to the Rector and Visitors of the University of Virginia, and I regret exceedingly the suggestion that led to it. I am very sensible of the kindness of the motive which prompted my friend to make the suggestion, and I shall never cease to remember with grateful pleasure this mark of confidence, from those whose confidence is, in my estimation, above all earthly price. But with very strong prepossessions towards the course of employment proposed to me, my situation compels me to decline it, and to resign myself, perhaps for life, to the more profitable labors of my profession... With the most grateful acknowledgments to the Rector and Visitors of the University of Virginia for the honor done me by an offer so flattering in all its circumstances, and with the personal kindness to me, dear sir, on this and every other occasion, I remain, as I have ever been,

Your faithful and devoted servant,
Wm. Wirt.[7]

When Wirt declined, John T. Lomax, a prominent Fredericksburg, Virginia attorney, was selected professor of law.

George Tucker, Wirt's friend and sometime literary collaborator, was given the chair of moral philosophy. As the eldest, Tucker was named first chairman. The University of Virginia would function without a President, as Jefferson had decreed, for the remainder of the century.[8]

In his letters, Wirt often talked about his wish to return to the relative tranquillity of the Blue Ridge Mountains where he had begun his career. Financial concerns and a desire to stay in the thick of things conspired to keep him where the big fees were. Had he acceded to the Board of Visitors' wishes and retired at age 54 to the halls of academe, perhaps Wirt would have prolonged his life and found time for more literary pursuits. Alas, it was not to be.

Jefferson died on July 4, 1826, at his home, Monticello, less than three months after his attempt to lure Wirt to Charlottesville. John Adams died the same day at his home in Quincy, Massachusetts, providing history with another strange coincidence. At the nation's capital, it was decided that the death of two men of such significance on the birthday of the Declaration of Independence demanded an appropriate eulogy. A ceremony was planned in the House of Representatives on October 19, the anniversary of Adams' birth and the British surrender at Yorktown. William Wirt was selected to deliver the eulogy. Wirt had no qualms about praising Jefferson, his old mentor. But, perhaps mindful of the flap he ignited among New Englanders with his biography of Patrick Henry, Wirt asked that another speaker handle Adams. The committee stuck to its plan, however, and Wirt acceded to their wishes. Dozens of distinguished orators, including Daniel Webster, John Tyler and Felix Grundy, were called upon to speak about Jefferson and Adams after their deaths, but it was Wirt who was selected to address Congress.[9]

As he prepared for this assignment, Wirt discussed Jefferson and the inevitability of death with his old friend Pope in a letter dated July 24, 1826: "Why, what a life it is! Before we can turn around three times we are old – and the servants call us 'old master' – and we hear our fellow travelers alluding to us as "-the old gentleman" – and the girls look away from us to ogle the boys, and tell us, as plain as looks can speak, that they would have none of us... What is the meaning of all this? I have not had my share of life's banquet yet – at least, my appetite is not satisfied... Plague on them all, I say! I am not old. Is a man old at fifty? Why Mr. Jefferson was fifty when he resigned the Secretaryship of State – and he was then not more than half way in his race either of enjoyment or glory... This fancy they have, of my being old, and treating me with the reverence due to age, is really quite diverting sometimes – and I catch myself laughing in my sleeve at their mistake... But the drollest part of the business is that my looking-glass seems to have fallen into the same mistake, reflecting gray whiskers, and a wrinkled forehead, and hair growing thin on the top and the crown of the head. This is carrying the joke too far... All I shall say is, that if old age really has come upon me I have lost a great deal of time in bashfulness and ceremony, and saving appearances, that might have been better employed... We must make haste to live to the best advantage – and crowd into every moment, all of utility, honor, and enjoyment that we can. This is the only true economy for such an evanescent life. I fancy Mr. Jefferson made the most of his."[10]

In his more than two-hour eulogy, Wirt chose a biographical structure and curbed his notorious flights of imagination except for when he came to the role both men played in the Declaration of Independence. Jefferson and Adams were not geniuses, Wirt declared, not "great and eccentric minds 'shot madly from their spheres' to affright the world and scatter pestilence in their course." Instead, they were "minds whose strong and steady light... came to cheer and to gladden a world." They were calm and reasonable men, men of common sense, who had been selected by Providence to guide the American people to independence. What Providence had given, Wirt said, it now, in an example of "moral sublimity," took away on the 50th anniversary of independence.

Americans could learn much about the lives of these two men, Wirt added. Both were highly cultivated products of regional cultures, the North and the South. Each was the spokesman of his "hemisphere." Adams represented the Puritanical spirit of a New England hardened by physical hardship. He was a master of self-discipline and schooled in political contention. Jefferson was the product of an aristocratic and chivalrous Virginia. Adams represented the American Sparta and Jefferson the American Athens, Wirt said. In obvious reference to the dispute he had stirred up with the elder Adams over the biography of Patrick Henry, Wirt proclaimed, "Whether Otis or Henry *first* breathed into this nation the breath of life (a question merely for curious and friendly speculation) it is very certain that they breathed into their two young hearers, that breath which has made them both immortal."[11]

Chapter 19

An Inspiration to Youth

Wirt never forgot the people who saw some potential in the young orphan from Bladensburg, Maryland, and went out of their way to prod and encourage him to make a success of himself. As a young adult, Wirt also benefited from mentors such as Jefferson, Madison and Monroe. Because of this experience, he devoted a great deal of time, energy and thought toward encouraging youngsters, whether relatives, friends or total strangers, to develop their mental faculties and make the most of their abilities. Many of Wirt's essays and much of his biography of Patrick Henry were designed to inspire youth and espouse the virtues of education. Wirt became a lawyer by watching successful attorneys in the Maryland courts and by reading the law under Fredericksburg, Virginia, lawyer Thomas Swann. In much the same way, many other young men learned the law under Wirt's tutelage.

Wirt had to scratch around for his education, working as a tutor and reading voraciously in the family libraries to which he had access. He encouraged all of his children, including his daughters, to develop their minds. In 1811, Wirt wrote the following passages of encouragement to his daughter Laura, who had just celebrated her eighth birthday:

"But we must not be like the man that prayed to Hercules to help his wagon out of the mud, and was too lazy to help himself – no, we must be thoughtful; try our very best to learn our books... Suppose there was a nest full of beautiful young birds, so young that they could not fly and help themselves, and they were opening their little mouths and crying for something to eat and drink, and their parents would not bring them any thing, but were to let them cry on from morning till night, till they starved and died; would they not be very wicked parents? Now, your mind is this nest full of beautiful little singing birds; much more beautiful and melodious than any canary birds in the world; and there sits fancy, and reason, and memory, and judgment – all with their little heads thrust forward out of the nest, and crying as hard as they can for something to eat and drink. Will you not love your father and mother for trying to feed them with books and learning, the only kind of meat and drink they love, and without which those sweet little songsters must, in a few years, hang their heads and die? ...You are very fond, when you get a new story book, of running through it as fast as you can, just for the sake of knowing what happened to this one, and that one; in doing this, you are feeding one of the four birds I have mentioned, that is *fancy,* which, to be sure, is the loudest singer among them, and will please you while you are young. But, while you are thus feeding and stuffing fancy – reason, memory and judgment are starving; and by-and-bye, you will think their notes much softer and sweeter than those of fancy... Therefore, you ought to feed those other birds as well."[1]

Another lawyer Wirt helped mold was Francis Walker Gilmer, the youngest brother of his first wife Mildred. Although Wirt left Charlottesville shortly after Mildred's death in 1799, he retained close ties with the Gilmer family. Wirt's relationship with young "Frank," whose father died when he was seven years old, was more that of big brother than brother-in-law. Dr. Gilmer's patient and friend, Thomas Jefferson, took a hand in guiding Francis Gilmer's education, as did Jefferson's confidant, Joseph Francisco Correa da Serra (the Abbe Correa). But it was in Wirt's Richmond law office that young Gilmer prepared for a career. Wirt continued to advise and encourage Gilmer in the law and literary pursuits, both of which he excelled in until his untimely death in 1826.[2]

On July 23, 1815, Wirt wrote to Gilmer, who was about to embark on his law career, saying, "You are to bear in mind that glory is not that easy kind of inheritance which the law will cast upon you, without any effort of your own; but that you are to work for it and fight for it... You are also to bear in mind, that the friends who know and love you, and acknowledge your talents, are not the world. That in regard to the world, upon which you are entering, you are an unknown... And that it is not by the display of your general science, that the herd is to be caught; but by the dexterity with which you handle your professional tools, and the power which you evince to serve your clients in your trade. Now, the law depends on such a system of unnatural reasoning, that your natural reasoning, however strong, will not serve the turn... But in the first place, you must read, sir: You must read and meditate, like a Conastoga horse – no disparagement to the horse by the simile. You must read like Jefferson, and speak like Henry... Don't make your first appearance in a trifling case. Get yourself either by a fee, or voluntarily, into the most important cause that is to be tried in Winchester, at the fall term... *level yourself* to the *capacity of your hearers*, and insinuate yourself among the heart-strings, the bones and marrow, both of your jury and back-bar hearers... One of the most dignified traits in the character of Henry, is the noble decorum with which he debated, and uniform and marked respect with which he treated his adversaries... Let it be universally agreed, that you are the most polite, gentlemanly debater at the bar. That alone will give you a distinction – and a noble one too..."[3]

Six weeks later, Wirt wrote Gilmer and urged him, "For two or three years, you must read, sir – read – read – delve – meditate – study – and make the whole mine of the law your own. For two or three years, I had much rather that your appearances should be rare and splendid, than frequent, light, and vapid, like those of the young country practitioners about you. Wirt added the following twelve-step program toward a successful beginning as a lawyer:

"1. Adopt a system of life, as to business and exercise; and never deviate from it, except so far as you may be occasionally forced by imperious and uncontrollable circumstances.

"2. Live in your office; i.e. be always seen in it except at the hours of eating or exercise.

"3. Answer all letters as soon as they are received; you know not how many heart-aches it may save you. Then fold neatly, endorse neatly, and file away neatly, alphabetically, and by the year, all the letters so received. Let your letters on business be short, and keep copies of them.

"4. Put every law paper in its place, as soon as received; and let no scrap of paper be seen laying for a moment on your writing chair or tables. This will strike the eye of every man of business who enters.

"5. Keep regular accounts of every cent of income and expenditure, and file your receipts neatly, alphabetically, and by the month, or at least by the year.

"6. Be patient with your foolish clients, and hear all their tedious circumlocution and repetitions with calm and kind attention; cross examine and sift them, 'till you know all the strength and weakness of their cause, and take notes of it at once whenever you can do so.

"7. File your bills in Chancery at the moment of ordering the suit, and while your client is yet with you to correct your statement of his case; also prepare every declaration the moment the suit is ordered, and have it ready to file.

"8. Cultivate a simple style of speaking, so as to be able to inject the strongest thought into the weakest capacity. You will never be a good jury lawyer without this faculty.

"9. Never attempt to be grand and magnificent before common tribunals – and the most you will address are common...

"10. Keep your Latin and Greek, and science to yourself, and to that very small circle which they might suit. The mean and envious world will never forgive you your knowledge if you make it too public...

"11. Enter with warmth and kindness into the interesting concerns of others – whether you care much for them or not – not with the condescension of a superior, but with the tenderness and simplicity of an equal. It is this benevolent trait which... more than anything else, has smoothed my own path of life, and strewed it with flowers.

"12. Be never flurried in speaking, but learn to assume the exterior of composure and self-collectedness, whatever riot and confusion may be within; speak slowly, distinctly, and mark your periods by proper pauses, and a steady significant look – 'Trick!' True – but a good trick, and a sensible trick.

"You see how natural it is for an old man to preach, and how much easier to preach than to practice. Yet you must not slight my sermons, for I wish you to be much greater than I ever was or can hope to be." [4]

In 1818, Wirt wrote to Gilmer, who had decided to come back to Richmond after three years in law practice in Winchester: "You will see that I oppose your removal to Richmond; but there is so much of *Providence* in these things, and so much depends on the *unvanquishable energy of the orator*, that human prudence becomes a pismire view of the subject. The die (as you say) is cast – and may Heaven prosper it! The step having been taken, all that remains is to make the best use of it:

"*1st.* Don't be in a hurry to distinguish yourself. And, on the other hand, don't hang back too long. Let the occasion of your first display be good, *and your preparation ripe.*

"*2d.* On all occasions, private and public, throw the utmost modesty, and the most scrupulous delicacy, into your manner, and be more disposed to have your scientific knowledge drawn from you than to volunteer a display of it.

"*3d. Read law like a horse.* Your friend Cabell will point out the best course to you. Pursue it indefatigably, and suffer no butterflies' wings, stones, &c., to draw you aside from it.

"*4th.* In your arguments at the bar, let *argument strongly predominate.* Sacrifice your flowers, and let your columns be doric, rather than composite – the better medium in Ionic. Avoid as you would the gates of death, the reputation of floridity. Small though your body, let the march of your mind be the stride of a seven-leagued giant.

"Aim at the character of *strength, cogency, comprehension,* and imitate, of all things, Judge Marshall's and Locke's simple process of reasoning. The world will ever give its sanction to this as the truest criterion of superior mind..." [5]

After he became Attorney General, Wirt ran his own informal school for would-be-lawyers. He had so many applicants that, in 1821, he drew up a set of regulations designed to weed out all but the most dedicated. It outlined a course of study similar to what St. George Tucker had devised at the College of William and Mary, and "described the written opinion on one subject and several oral arguments on others each student must present, and listed some of the reading in history and belles-lettres to be done in the evenings," according to Davis. The hours of study were listed as 9 a.m. to 3 p.m. in the summer and 10 a.m. to 3 p.m. in the winter. When not in court, Wirt made himself available during these hours to answer questions. [6]

To another of his law students, S. Treakle Wallis, Wirt said, "It will no longer do to fill the ear only with pleasant sounds, or the fancy with fine images. The mind, the understanding must be filled with solid thought. The age of ornament is over: that of utility has succeeded. The *pugnae quam pompae aptius* is the order of the day, and men fight now with clenched fist, not with the open hand – with logic and not with rhetoric... The great herd of mankind, the *fruges consumere nati* pass their lives in listless inattention and indifference as to what is going on around them, being perfectly content to satisfy the mere cravings of nature, while those who are destined for distinction have a lynx-eyed vigilance that nothing can escape." [7]

Shortly before his death, Wirt answered a letter from a student at Chapel Hill, North Carolina, advising him to "never be satisfied with the surface of things: probe them to the bottom, and let nothing go 'till you understand it as thoroughly as your powers will enable you. Seize the moment of excited curiosity on any subject, to solve your doubts; for if you let it pass, the desire may never return, and you may remain in ignorance... With regard to the style of eloquence you should adopt, that must depend very much on your own taste and genius... The ape alone is content with mere imitation."[8]

Among those who learned the law under Wirt were Abel P. Upshur, Secretary of State under John Tyler, William C. Preston, Dolley Madison's god-child who became a U.S. Senator and John Pendleton Kennedy who in 1849 wrote the two volume, *Memoirs of the Life of William Wirt, Attorney General of the United States.* Kennedy's biographer Charles H. Bohner said Kennedy so admired his mentor that he patterned his life after him, seeking fame "in the three fields in which Wirt was popularly conceded to excel all other men in the Union: law, literature and oratory." Wirt called Kennedy "a right merry young lawyer," and exerted influence on James Monroe to name Kennedy Secretary to the Legation to Chile. Kennedy's 1832 novel, *Swallow Barn,* which is dedicated to Wirt, is often cited as the first successful Southern novel, or plantation novel. Bohner noted that Wirt may have seen some of himself in "Philly Wart," one of Swallow Barn's Characters. Although he praised the book in public, Wirt confided to Dabney Carr, "it is a *non-descript* sort of a novel... flippant and smart enough, but no deep and strong drawing or solemnizing... I am complimented by the dedication, it would seem ungrateful in me to decry the work." Like Wirt, Kennedy married well. In 1840, he and his wife, Elizabeth Gray Kennedy, purchased the Wirt's house on Baltimore's fashionable Monument Square. Kennedy became known as a novelist, historian, lawyer and orator. He served two separate terms in Congress, was speaker of the Maryland House of Delegates and served in Millard Fillmore's cabinet as Secretary of the Navy.[9]

Wirt's influence was not limited to young lawyers. In 1829, Wirt was approached by a young Edgar Allan Poe asking him to read a poem, *Al Aaraaf,* and offer an opinion. Befuddled by the style, Wirt diplomatically suggested that Poe seek more expert advice: "I am sensible of the compliment you pay me in submitting it to my judgment and only regret that you have not a better counselor. But the truth is that having never written poetry myself, nor read much poetry for many years, I consider myself as by no means a competent judge.... It will, I know, please modern readers... I should doubt whether the poem will take with old fashioned readers like myself. But this will be of little consequence..."[10]

Perhaps the most famous of the young lawyers who studied under Wirt was Salmon P. Chase, who presided over the Kansas-Nebraska debate in the Senate and sought the Presidency before and after the Civil War. During the heat of the furor over slavery, Chase remembered Wirt as a kindly slave owner, calling him "one of the purest and noblest of men." [11] A vehement opponent of slavery, Chase was once known as "the attorney general for runaway slaves." He was elected to the U.S. Senate from Ohio in 1849, resigning his seat in 1855 to become Governor of Ohio. Chase was reelected to the Senate in 1861, but resigned two days after being seated to join Lincoln's cabinet as Secretary of the Treasury. In that capacity, he pulled the federal government out of bankruptcy by issuing "greenbacks" and setting up the National Banking System, which regulated monetary affairs until the Federal Reserve Act of 1913. Chase was appointed Chief Justice of the Supreme Court in 1864 and presided over the impeachment trial of President Andrew Johnson. Chase served as Chief Justice until his death in 1873.

In 1830, Wirt addressed the Peithessophian and Philoclean societies of Rutgers College on the value of education, saying, "Suffer me, in the first place, to call your attention to the power of the great magician – education – in forming and directing the human character... the Education, moral and intellectual, of every individual, must be chiefly his own work. There is a prevailing and a fatal mistake on this subject. It seems to be supposed that if a young man be sent first to a grammar school, and then to college, he must, of course become a scholar: and that the pupil himself is apt to imagine that he is to be the mere passive recipient of instruction, as he is of the light and atmosphere which surrounds him." Wirt urged his listeners to embark on a lifelong quest for knowledge that will never be totally fulfilled: "Our happiness is never present but always in the prospect. We are, constantly, reaching forward to some object ahead of us, which we flatter ourselves we will fill ... Thus, Hope cheats us on, from point to point, and, at the close of a long life, however successful it may have been, we find that we have been chasing meteors which have dissolved at the touch." [12]

Chapter 20

End of an Era

By the autumn of 1828, it became apparent that Andrew Jackson would succeed in his quest for the presidency. This would be no mere change in leadership, but the end of an administrative dynasty begun by Jefferson in 1800. The Democrat-Republicans had ruled in the nation's capital for more than a generation. Jefferson, Madison and Monroe were all Virginians, and John Quincy Adams, who had served Monroe as Secretary of State, continued the philosophical lineage. Old Hickory, however, was a different breed of cat. A Jackson victory would represent only the second shift of power in the young nation's history, and there was no precedent on how the transition would affect Cabinet officers. Wirt, at least, had a question in his mind about this, especially since he had attempted to be apolitical. He asked Monroe for advice on this matter:

"Whether the present administration ought to withdraw, in the event of Mr. Adams not being re-elected, is a question of great delicacy as to the members, and of interest, by way of example, as to principle. They hold their offices as others do, as servants of the public, not the President's," Monroe replied. "In some views, therefore, they may be considered as holding an independent ground: that is, as depending on their good conduct in office, and not on the change of the incumbent. In others, the opposite argument appears to have force. When a difference of principle is involved, it would seem as if a change would be necessary... Your duties are different. The President has less connection with and less responsibility for the performance of them. Your standing is, likewise, such – nothing unfriendly having occurred between you – that I should think he (General Jackson) would wish to retain you."[1]

Neither Wirt nor Monroe fully appreciated Jackson's way of doing business. When the old Indian fighter came to

Washington, he cleaned house, installing his own people in key positions. Wirt was out of a job, but not without prospects. During his time as Attorney General, his private client base went from local to national. Wirt toyed briefly with moving his practice to New York, before settling on Baltimore. In the days before Jackson's inauguration, Wirt discussed his decision with his old friend, Judge Carr: "My wife, on a full view of the whole ground, gives the preference to Baltimore. She is delighted to get away from the threatening storm and from the new association here – and my children are all reconciled to it." Wirt expressed few regrets about leaving office and returning to the state in which he was born. "As Erskine said, when they turned him out of the office of Chancellor, 'I am much obliged to them, for they have given me, in exchange for a dog's life, that of a gentleman,'" Wirt wrote Carr.[2]

To his friend William Pope, Wirt wrote: "The office I have held for the last twelve years, I have filled without discredit to my country or myself – I hope with some honor to both. I leave it without a single reproach even from my enemies – if I have any – and with the respect, I might say the affection, of the Supreme Court... The General, I fear, is in the hands of two or three most miserable advisors – private and not official advisors, I mean. Some of his appointments for the cabinet have astounded the more enlightened part of his political supporters. One of them has been heard to say, 'This is the Millennium of Minnows'... It is a matter of relief both to my family and myself to get away from such a scene of contention and confusion... The more I see of public life the more sick I become of it, and the more deeply I am convinced that all is vanity and vexation of spirit beyond the happy domestic and social circle." Leaving his duties as Attorney General after nearly 12 years on the job had no appreciable effect on the hectic pace Wirt set for himself. "I shall have a busy summer, for I have to argue a cause in Boston, about the twentieth of June, and must hurry back to the Court of Appeals in Maryland. I am not likely to rust from inactivity," he told Pope.[3]

Wirt was impressed with Massachusetts on his visit there in 1829. Although his sometime ally Webster was his opponent in the case there, the two lawyers spent much time together outside the courtroom. "Boston, seen in the approach and with all its revolutionary associations, is the most beautiful and interesting picture I have ever beheld. New York is not to compare with it; even our beautiful Richmond, dearly and tenderly as I love it, sinks under comparison," Wirt wrote Judge

Cabell. "I walked through the town last night, with Webster, by moonlight, and was quite overwhelmed with the air of wealth exhibited in the vast number of granite and brick palaces which abound through the place... This is certainly the most hospitable place in the world." The case that brought Wirt to argue before the Massachusetts Supreme Court (Henry Farnum, administrator, of Tuthill Hubbart, v. Peter C. Brooks) was a dry affair, but Wirt relished the prospect of winning it and besting Webster: "It is an old insurance account, of forty years standing, and I am following the explanations of one of the truest-nosed beagles that ever was put upon a cold trial. He is a fine fellow and as true as a rifle; and it is quite a curiosity to see him threading these old mazes... I am brought here to combat Webster on his own arena – and I think I shall gain the day, which will be a great triumph."[4]

While in Boston, Wirt picked up a new client in the Warren Bridge case. He returned to Annapolis, Maryland, to argue in a controversy between the Chesapeake and Ohio Canal and the Rail Road Company of Baltimore, but he continued to talk about his trip to Boston to his friends. The experience had purged him of some Mid-Atlantic prejudices toward Yankees. "...I say they are as warm-hearted, as kind, as frank, as truly hospitable as the Virginians themselves. In truth, they are Virginians in all the essentials of character," he wrote Judge Carr. "Would to Heaven the people of Virginia and Massachusetts, knew each other better! ... What a fool have I been to join in these vulgar prejudices against the Yankees! We judged them by our peddlers."[5]

One of Wirt's most celebrated appearances after leaving the office of Attorney General was in the impeachment hearing of Judge James H. Peck in 1830. Appointed a District Court Judge in the Missouri territory by the Monroe Administration, Peck was accused of highhanded disregard for legal procedures by Luke Edward Lawless, a lawyer Peck had jailed for a day in 1826 and suspended from practice for 18 months. Lawless was unsuccessful in seeking redress through several sessions of Congress, but persisted. The issue became a political football and Lawless and Peck both aired their sides in the partisan press. In December, 1829, Peck was impeached by the newly-elected "Jacksonian" House of Representatives, by a vote of 123-49. Wirt was hired to represent Peck in the Senate hearing.

Although the judge had many differences of opinion with occupants of the bench during his own forty-year legal career, Wirt characterized Peck as a fair, but firm justice who had a difficult job to do in the Wild West: "Suppose a judge (I put it, for the present, hypothetically) in a distant and frontier territory to have thrown upon him, by the legislature of his country, the judicial settlement of a vast mass of foreign land claims, held partly by the original claimants, chiefly by sharp-sighted and sharp-set speculators, of rapacious and insatiable appetite; among which claims, though there were, no doubt, some that were fair and honest, there were others of a false and fraudulent character, which their holders might attempt to force through his tribunal by their intrepidity and effrontery – I appeal to every considerate man whether such a judge is not placed in a situation which calls upon him to hold the reins of authority with a strong and firm hand, and to rebuke, with promptitude and energy, the first attempt to insult or to intimidate his tribunal? ... We insist that Judge Peck has done no more than every judge would have had the perfect right and power to do under a similar attack upon the authority of his tribunal."[6]

Lawless, Wirt said, took out his frustrations by attacking the judge after he saw his case, and the promise of additional lucrative fees, go down the drain. "If he be an irritable man, a man of turbulent and lawless propensities, a man used to the wild uproar of insurrection and civil war, his first impulse will probably be revenge upon the tribunal which has inflicted the disappointment ... Or, if he looked deeper into the game, he might have concerted a plan of hostilities, of which this libel was to be the first stroke, to blow up the tribunal altogether, and to erect another upon its ruin, before which his shattered troop of claims might appear with renovated hopes." Wirt handily dispatched Lawless' contention that because he spoke with an Irish accent and used many foreign terms, Judge Peck misinterpreted him: "An honorable manager has told us that Mr. Lawless is an Irishman, and when he said *prohibit*, he meant *not authorize*. An Englishman would not be apt to call *capers, anchovies*, and shoot a brother officer through the head for doubting his assertion that they grew on trees."[7]

In considering Judge Peck, Wirt said, the Senate must look at the larger picture. "It is the question of the independence of the American judiciary. It is in his person that that independence is sought to be violated. Is this Court prepared to suspend the sword by a hair over the heads of our judges, and constrain them to the performance of their duties amidst fear and trembling from the terrors of an impeachment? ... Can you, by such a precedent, strike a panic throughout the American bench, and fill the bosoms of all the reflecting, the wise and good, with dismay and despair? Sir, there is not a considerate man who has not long regarded a pure, firm, enlightened judiciary as the great sheet-anchor of our national constitution. Snap the cable that binds us to that, and farewell to our Union and the yet dawning glories of our Republic."[8]

A two-third's majority of the Senate was necessary for conviction. After six weeks of debate, the Senate voted 22-21 against conviction. Judge Peck was acquitted of all charges against him. It is ironic that Peck's defender was William Wirt, who as a young lawyer in 1800 had stomped out of the courtroom in protest of the imperious demeanor of Judge Samuel Chase. Still, the exoneration of Judge Peck, who had been vilified by the pro-Jackson press, was a satisfying victory for Wirt.

Chapter 21

The Cherokee Cases

T wo of the most notable cases Wirt tried after leaving the post of Attorney General involved the Cherokee Nation's claims against the State of Georgia. In the *Letters of A British Spy,* a youthful Wirt decried the treatment of Native Americans at the hands of the European settlers, although he somewhat ingeniously blamed the British for setting up an unjust system that the United States inherited and could do little to rectify. (He had often used the same justification for owning slaves while despising the institution of slavery.) But in the Cherokee claims, Wirt was able to develop fully his sympathies for the Native Americans and effectively argue that they possessed rights that both preceded and superseded the rights of individual states.

Since the early 1800s, Georgia officials had lobbied to do away with the Cherokee lands within their state's borders. Unlike many tribes, however, the Cherokees had been notably successful in resisting these attempts to push them off their ancestral homelands. The Cherokees were also the most willing to adopt many modern ways and by the 1820s, had set up a prosperous society, complete with a Constitution patterned after that of the United States, schools, a newspaper and a written language. They took seriously the concept of nationhood, much to the irritation of Georgians desirous of their land. The Constitution of the Cherokee Nation, adopted in 1827, created an illegal state within a state, the Georgians asserted, citing the new states clause of the federal Constitution (Art. VI, sec. 3).[1]

Given the considerable sympathy among many Americans for the plight of the Indian tribes, Georgia's initiative would have been doomed but for two significant factors. The first was the election to the Presidency of legendary "Indian fighter" Andrew Jackson in 1828. The second was the discovery of gold in the Cherokee lands in 1829. The combination of greed and an ally in the White House prompted the Georgians to redouble their efforts to drive the Cherokees out of their state. Georgia extended its criminal jurisdiction over the Cherokee Nation, outlawed tribal council meetings, barred Cherokees from testifying in state courts and nullified the Constitution of the Cherokee Nation. In February, 1830, Jackson supporters in Congress introduced a bill to move the Cherokees west of the Mississippi. After an acrimonious and protracted battle, the bill became law.[2]

Prompted by both moral indignation and political motivation, many National Republicans seized Old Hickory's Indian policies as an issue. Daniel Webster and Henry Clay organized petition campaigns to repeal the bill in Congress. Webster and others urged the Cherokees to take their case before the Supreme Court, recommending William Wirt as legal counsel. As one of the most experienced lawyers in the nation and the former Attorney General, Wirt seemed an ideal choice. Because he had little love for Jackson and was intensely sympathetic to the Native American cause, Wirt was sure to pursue the case with vigor. Realistically, Wirt knew the President was unlikely to enforce a court decision favoring the Indians. If Jackson could be shown to be a tyrant who ignored the law and the Supreme Court, however, it could have an impact on the upcoming presidential election.

Wirt wrote to Georgia Governor George Gilmer, a distant relative of Wirt's first wife, asking cooperation in settling the Cherokees' case. Gilmer responded by accusing Wirt of using family ties to influence an internal state matter and labeling the Supreme Court as a biased tribunal – a stance shared by many of Jackson's supporters. With the battle lines drawn, the matter went before the high court in June, 1830. When the Cherokees and Creeks refused to be relocated, Jackson dismissed them by saying, "We have answered that we leave them ... to the protection of their friend Mr. Wirt... The course of Wirt had been truly wicked... I have used all the persuasive means in my power... and now leave the poor deluded Creeks and Cherokees to their wicked advisors."[3]

The Cherokees, Wirt argued before the court, were distinct among all of the Native Americans in their willingness to live in harmony with those of European descent: "Through a long course of years, they have followed our counsel with the docility of children. Our wish has been their law. We asked them to be civilized, and they became so. They assumed our dress, copied our names, pursued our course of education, adopted our form of government, embraced our religion, and have been proud to imitate us in every thing in their power... They have even adopted our resentments, and in our war with the Seminole tribes, they voluntarily joined our arms and gave effectual aid in driving back those barbarians from the very State that now oppresses them... They fought side by side with our present Chief Magistrate, and received his repeated thanks for their gallantry and conduct. ...they have refused us no gratification which it has been in their power to grant. We asked them for a portion of their lands, and they ceded it. We asked them again and again, and they continued to cede, until they have now reduced themselves within the narrowest compass that their own subsistence will permit... We promised them, and they trusted us: Shall they be deceived... Is this the high mark to which the American nation has been so strenuously and successfully pressing forward? Shall we sell the mighty meed of our high honors at so worthless a price, and in two short years, cancel all the glory which we have been gaining before the world for the last half century? ...If truth and faith and honor and justice have fled from every other part of our country, we shall find them here. If not – our sun has gone down, in treachery, blood and crime, in the face of the world; and instead of being proud of our country, as heretofore, we may well call upon the rocks and mountains to hide our shame from earth and heaven."[4]

Wirt argued that the many treaties signed between the Cherokee Nation and the federal government recognized the right of sovereign status and the propriety of the Cherokees' appeal to the Supreme Court:

"How is the question of the political condition of these people to be settled? I know of no other mode of doing it than by an appeal to their history. Looking at this history, we find that they composed a part of the *aboriginal* inhabitants of this country, and in their origin, they were unquestionably *a sovereign people, owing allegiance to no other earthly potentate.*" European settlement, Wirt argued, altered the change of Indian title to a portion of their lands, through sale or barter, but this did not alter "the *political condition* of these people. With regard to their lands, they were admitted, says Chief Justice Marshall, in the case of Johnson and MacIntosh, '*to be rightful occupants of the soil, with a legal as well as just claim to retain the possession of it, and to use it according to their own discretion;*' and with regard to their political condition, Great Britain, the prior discoverer of this part of the continent, continually *treated* with these people, as a *sovereign people*, and acknowledged in practice, as well as theory, their exclusive right to govern themselves by their own laws, usages and customs... The same right which had been held by Great Britain, and no other, passed to the United States by the Revolution; and the same rights and no others have been uniformly asserted by the United States. The various treaties which have been set forth... and to which the State of Georgia as one of the United States was a party, contains the most unequivocal admissions, that *these people are not citizens of the United States,* and *therefore cannot be citizens of any one of the states;* that the territory within which they dwell, *belongs to them* as a separate people; that *within this territory,* they are the sovereign and only lawgivers."[5]

In summary, Wirt argued: That "the Cherokees are a sovereign nation and their having placed themselves under the protection of the United States does not at all impair their sovereignty and independence as a nation; "That the territory of the Cherokees is not within the jurisdiction of the State of Georgia, but within the sole and exclusive jurisdiction of the Cherokee Nation; That, consequently, the State of Georgia has no right to extend her laws over that territory.

Wirt further argued:

That, the law of Georgia which has been placed before me, is unconstitutional and void. 1. Because it is repugnant to the treaties between the United States and the Cherokee Nation. 2. Because it is repugnant to a law of the United States passed in 1802, entitled "an act to regulate trade and intercourse with the Indian tribes, and to preserve peace on the frontiers. 3. Because it is repugnant to the Constitution, inasmuch as it impairs the obligations of all the contracts arising under the treaties with the Cherokees; and affects moreover, to regulate intercourse with an Indian tribe, a power which belongs, exclusively, to Congress."[6]

In reference to Georgia's refusal to recognize the authority of the Court and Jackson's sympathy for the state's stance, Wirt argued, "In a land of laws, the presumption is that the decisions of the Court will be respected; and, in case they should not, it is a poor government indeed in which there does not exist power to enforce respect... what is the value of that government in which the decrees of its courts can be mocked at and defied with impunity? ... It is no government at all... In pronouncing your decree you will have declared law; and it is part of the sworn duty of the President of the United States to 'take care that the laws be faithfully executed.' ...If he refuses to perform his duty, the Constitution has provided a remedy."[7]

Then in his 29th year as Chief Justice, John Marshall had considerable sympathy for the plight of the Cherokees. But he also knew which way political winds were blowing in Washington, D.C. Marshall was unwilling to give Wirt and his supporters an excuse to impeach President Jackson. Marshall dismissed the case for want of jurisdiction. He ruled that the Cherokee Nation was not a sovereign state, but a domestic dependent nation, likening the relationship to that of a ward and his guardian. But in so ruling, Marshall left the door open for another case on Indian rights. He said that the interposition of the Court under the circumstances of *The Cherokee Nation v. Georgia* smacked too much of the "exercise of political power." A question based on Cherokee property or personal rights, however, "might perhaps be decided by this Court in a proper case with proper parties," Marshall stated.[8]

The next year, Wirt was back before the Supreme Court in *Worcester v. Georgia.* Wirt appeared on behalf of Samuel A. Worcester, one of seven missionaries who had been convicted for violating a Georgia law that prohibited whites from residing on Cherokee land. Five of the missionaries accepted a deal which granted them a pardon in return for agreeing to conform to the state laws. Worcester and Elizur Butler stuck by their principles and were sentenced to four years of hard labor in the Georgia Penitentiary. The law in question was an outgrowth of a general belief that the missionaries were an impediment to a government plan to bribe the Cherokee into giving up their lands and moving West.[9]

In this case, Wirt was more successful. Marshall and a majority of the court ruled that the Georgia statute was an unconstitutional infringement of the federal government's exclusive control over Indian affairs. "The Cherokee Nation, then, is a distinct community, occupying its own territory, with boundaries accurately described, in which the laws of Georgia can have no force, and which the citizens of Georgia have no right to enter but with the assent of the Cherokees themselves or in conformity with treaties and with the acts of Congress," Marshall wrote. "The act of the State of Georgia under which the plaintiff in error was prosecuted is consequently void, and the judgment a nullity.... The Acts of Georgia are repugnant to the Constitution, laws, and treaties of the United States.... The forcible seizure and abduction of the plaintiff, who was residing in the nation with its permission, and by authority of the President of the United States, is also a violation of the acts which authorize the chief magistrate to exercise this authority,"

Marshall wrote in overturning the Georgia Court's judgment. and ordering the prisoners' release.[10] Defiant, Georgia Governor Gilmer refused to comply with the court order, saying he would rather hang the two unfortunate missionaries than release them under the Supreme Court's mandate. Incensed by the court's decision, Jackson snapped, "John Marshall has made his decision. Now let him enforce it!"[11] Under the cloak of Presidential inaction, Georgia held out for 18 months before capitulating and releasing Worcester and Butler.[12]

The Cherokee cases of 1830-31 are viewed by many as a fight for the protection of the Constitution against the concept of states' rights, an issue that featured prominently in the 1832 presidential election. As the defender of the Cherokees' Constitutional rights, Wirt's name appeared as a possible vice presidential candidate on an anti-Jackson ticket. In August, 1831, the Pennsylvania National Republicans unanimously recommended Henry Clay as the presidential candidate and Wirt as his running mate.[13]

Chapter 22

Wirt for President

As William Wirt approached his 60th year, the man who had spurned many offers to seek elective office throughout his adult life found himself a candidate for the highest office in the land. Wirt was nominated for the Presidency by the Anti-Masonic Party, a group of sincere, though misguided, zealots who hoped to head off a second term for Andrew Jackson while furthering their rather narrow cause.

Wirt was no fan of "Old Hickory." It was Jackson who stood outside the courtroom in Richmond during the Burr Trial, stirring up the rabble against the prosecution and labeling Burr's prosecution as nothing more than a cheap political trick of Jefferson's. Years later, as a member of Monroe's cabinet, Wirt had opposed the old Indian fighter's shenanigans in Florida. And it was Jackson who booted Wirt out of the office of Attorney General after a comfortable 12 years on the job. But his opposition to Jackson had deeper roots. Although Wirt was a self-made man who once flirted with the notion of heading west to Kentucky to seek his fortune, he had, instead, stayed in Virginia and energetically modeled himself after the cultured, sophisticated and well-read Virginia gentry. Semiliterate roughnecks like Jackson and the bulk of his followers were distasteful to Wirt and many other followers of Jefferson. Wirt's feverish attempt in *Sketches* to give Patrick Henry more intellectual credentials than the patriot possessed and his constant harping to his children and other young men and women about the importance of a classical education cast Wirt and Jackson on philosophically opposite sides, regardless of their political differences.

Baltimore was the scene of two political conventions in 1831. As early as May, the Whigs in Wirt's congressional district asked the former Attorney General to represent them as a delegate. Henry Clay was seen as the best bet to deny Jackson a second term, and Wirt had expressed his leanings toward Clay, who had been Secretary of State during Wirt's years in John

Quincy Adams's cabinet. "We are, you know, to have a great National Convention here in December, and I have been asked to represent this district in it," Wirt wrote his old friend Judge Carr. "Now I hate politics, and can never be a party man – much less a party leader – for 'I trust I have a good conscience;' and, in these times I doubt the practicability of a politician possessing such a blessing. Besides, I have not the nerve to bear the vulgar abuse which is the politician's standing dish... if the people wish me to go to the Convention in December, I will go and utter their sentiments... At present, I think Clay the soundest amongst the candidates, and that he will make a good President... My friends here talk of making it a stepping stone to the Senate of the United States. But what do I care for the Senate? I am rather too old to start now, for the first time, on such a course, and have neither speed nor bottom for the race."[1]

In other sections of the country, the opposition to Jackson was assuming different forms. The Anti-Masonic movement had built up a considerable following in Pennsylvania, New York and New England, propelled by a furor over the mysterious disappearance of William Morgan in upstate New York. Once a Mason, Morgan had betrayed his lodge brothers by publishing Masonic secrets for profit. It was widely believed that Morgan had been abducted and murdered by Masons. In the election of 1828, Anti-Masons in New York joined forces with Adams' supporters but nominated their own candidate for Governor. Although Anti-Masonry was seen by most as an isolated aberration, Morgan's murder and a general feeling that the Masons were an elitist organization was used to whip up anti-Masonic feelings throughout the Northeast as the 1832 election approached. Neither Jackson nor Clay, both Masons, were palatable to the Anti-Masons, who doggedly scheduled their own third-party convention at the Baltimore Athenaeum in late September, 1831, a full two months before the Whigs were to gather. Several well-known politicians including Adams were approached as candidates and declined. When Supreme Court Justice John McLean abruptly withdrew his name from nomination, the Anti-Masons looked around for another prominent man and settled on Wirt, who had never expressed anti-Masonic sentiment, but lived just a few blocks away from the convention hall. Much to his surprise, Wirt's name was placed into nomination as the Anti-Masonic Candidate for President. He received 108 of the 111 delegate votes. On the motion of Thaddeus Stevens, Wirt was declared the unanimous choice by acclamation. Pennsylvanian Amos Ellmaker was the nominee for Vice President.[2]

Though befuddled by the honor, Wirt graciously accepted. In a hastily-drafted message to the convention, Wirt noted, "Not only have I never sought the office, but I have long since looked at it with far more of dread, than of desire, being fully aware of its fearful responsibilities, and of the fact, demonstrated by past experience, that no degree of purity and intelligence that can be exerted in the discharge of its duties, can protect its possessor from misrepresentation and aspersion."[3]

Wirt very quickly set his enthusiastic supporters straight as to his feelings on Masonry, however: "You must understand, then, if you are not already apprised of it, that in very early life, I was myself initiated into the mysteries of Free Masonry. I have been told by Masons that my eyes were not opened, because I never took the Master's degree; but my curiosity never led me thus far – and, although, I soon discontinued my attendance on lodges, (not having entered one even from curiosity for more than thirty years, I believe,) it proceeded from no suspicion on my part that there was anything criminal in the institution, or anything that placed its members, in the slightest degree, in collision with their allegiance to their country and its laws... I have, thenceforward, continually regarded masonry as nothing more than a social and charitable club, designed for the promotion of good feeling among its members, and for the pecuniary relief of their indigent brethren... Thinking thus of it, nothing has surprised me than to see it blown into consequence, in the Northern and Eastern States, as a political engine, and the whole community excited against it as an affair of serious importance... I have repeatedly and continually, both in conversation and letters of friendship, spoken of Masonry and Anti-Masonry, as a fitter subject for farce than tragedy... If, with these views of my opinions, it is the pleasure of your Convention to change the nomination, I can assure you very sincerely that I shall retire from it with far more pleasure than I should accept it."[4]

The following day, Wirt sent a newspaper clipping of the convention story to Judge Carr, adding, "you will see that I have been drawn into a political scrape, which has taken me as much by surprise as if a thunderbolt had dropped at my feet in a clear day... I have kept aloof all my life, from such affairs, and would have blessed my stars if I could have been let alone now." Wirt also hinted that he saw his nomination more as a means of defeating Jackson than as a method of promoting Anti-Masonry.

"It is a perfectly new move on the chess-board to intriguing politicians of all parties, and must perplex them at first. In such a matter people cannot be perplexed without exasperation. It is no move of mine, however – so that if it be deep and puzzling, the credit is not with me. I believe it to be perfectly simple and honest. If I did not believe so, I certainly would have nothing to do with it. I have been and still am friendly to Mr. Clay..."[5]

Wirt amplified this theme in a letter to Salmon P. Chase, dated November 11, 1831: "Considering the strength of their party [the Anti-Masons] and the rapidity with which it was increasing, I saw at once that unless we could secure their nomination for Mr. Clay, we could not elect him." But in conversations with the Anti-Masons, Wirt told Chase, he determined that they had approached Clay to see if he would turn his back on the Masonic order and accept their nomination and that Clay had refused. "I asked him how it would be possible for Mr. Clay, situated as he was before the public, to come out in such a way, without subjecting himself to the most invidious constructions? I added that he would be charged with having renounced his Masonic fraternity, for the sordid purpose of buying up their nomination..." Wirt wrote Chase. The Anti-Masons told him, Wirt added, that most of their supporters in Pennsylvania "were originally and still Jackson men, and, Anti-Masonry out of the way would return to Jackson. That it was absurd to think these men would leave Jackson because he was a Royal Arch, and unite on Mr. Clay who was a High Priest." Wirt vowed to Chase that he would not let the Anti-Masons turn him into a "politician," although he would let them make him President. "I shall not change my manners; they are a part of my nature. If the people choose to take me as I am – well. If not, they will only leave me where I have always preferred to be, enjoying the independence of private life. They may make some rents in my garments in the meantime, but they will make none, I hope, in my peace of mind."[6]

Although he only hinted at it his letters, the possibility that he might emerge as the candidate of both the Anti-Masonic and Whig parties had to be in the back of Wirt's mind. Realizing that Clay, a Mason, could not possibly take an estimated 500,000 Anti-Mason votes (a wildly optimistic appraisal), perhaps the Whigs would seek a united challenge to Jackson. As a protégé of Jefferson, Madison and Monroe, Wirt was solidly in the Whig camp. Kennedy, who studied law under Wirt, theorized that his mentor would have been more than willing to step down from his role as the Anti-Masonic standard bearer if the Whigs chose someone other than Clay.[7] As it turned out, however, events were cast in stone. At the National Republican Convention in December, also held in Baltimore's Athenaeum, Henry Clay received the votes of all but one delegate and was made the unanimous choice by acclamation.[8]

As the Whigs were preparing to meet, Wirt expressed little disappointment in his failure to unite the two parties in a letter to Judge Carr, dated December 5, 1831: "There seems to be no doubt of Mr. Clay's nomination by the Convention here next Wednesday. So be it. In a personal point of view, I shall feel that I have made a lucky escape. I told the Anti-Masons that they had rung the knell of my departed peace. I am relieved by seeing that I am likely to be reprieved. It is supposed, I have no doubt, that I shall be mortified by the rejection. How little do they know of me! A culprit pardoned at the gallows could not be more light-hearted... It has been suggested to me by a clergyman, that the Presbyterians are thinking of coming to my aid. I belong to their church. They are said to number a hundred and twenty thousand votes. My advice to them is, to stick to their religion, and not to sully it by mixing in political strife. They will make more hypocrites than Christians by such a course. This is bad advice as a politician, but sound as a Christian."[9]

Although not committed to being a candidate, Wirt was committed to defeating Jackson in any way possible. Later in his letter to Carr, Wirt commented on the President's latest speech, which he assumed was written by an aide and termed, "a well-concocted dish. If the Government was to be administered by messages, we should do well enough... What a varnish we have here of a sepulchre full of corruption... How is the treatment of the poor Indians white-washed... The President acts as if he supposed the Constitution *enjoined* a double term and the appointment of members [to Congress], and as if he required a constitutional *prohibition* to prevent him from doing what he declares to be wrong in principle."[10]

During the last weeks of 1831 and the first weeks of 1832, Wirt suffered from an attack of erysipelas brought on by a cold and overwork. Perhaps realizing he was the standard bearer for a lost cause, Wirt attempted to use his poor physical condition as the reason for a graceful withdrawal from the election, while still hoping to swing the Anti-Masonic block to Clay. In a letter to Carr dated January 12, 1832, Wirt told his old friend about his lack of success in this endeavor. "I cannot tell you how much

I am amused at the simplicity and single-heartedness of your proposal to the Anti-Masons to go over to Clay. I do most devoutly wish they would do it; but there is no more chance for Clay with the Anti-Masons 'than for the Pope of Rome.' " Wirt told Carr that he had approached party leaders, assuring them that he had no desires to be President, and that his "paramount wish was to see the government rescued out of the hands that now held the reins."[11]

Although he refused to dignify his nomination by the Anti-Masons by engaging in vigorous campaigning, by the autumn of 1832, Wirt was still holding to a faint hope that he could play a deciding role in the Electoral College if he managed to steer enough votes away from Jackson. On October 25, 1832, Wirt wrote Judge Carr, dismissing his friend's hopes that he might become president, "It will be a strange affair if it should happen. But I have no thought of it. 'The game is, certainly, within the power of the dice.' But it requires so many fortunate throws in succession, that it would be next to a miracle to win... I have never believed, since that nomination, that the opposition would succeed. I do not believe it now... Like you, I have sometimes hopes – not for myself – but for Clay. If he can but lead up the Western States handsomely, and we can save Pennsylvania and New York from the grasp of the administration, we may bring him in. My opinion is that the election ought not to be permitted to go before the House. If Clay can get the votes he counts on, he ought to be elected by a union in the electoral college. If I can effect this, it shall be done. I have no idea of suffering myself to be thrust before the House of Representatives for their votes, and I will prevent it if I can."[12]

Jackson's supporters attempted to style Wirt as little more than "an Old Federalist," a charge to which the Anti-Masonic press responded sharply. Wirt was "the favorite of Jefferson, the cherished friend of Madison, the chosen counselor of Monroe," Thurlow Weed wrote in the Albany *Evening Journal.* "The fame of the great man should be cherished... it ought to be preserved as an example for our youth to imitate – for our nation to reverence, and for other nations to respect," the *Rhode Island American* pontificated. Wirt's supporters said his strong ties to the republicanism and intellectual enlightenment of Jefferson and Madison made him just the man to stop America's slide into corruption and despair, a theme that Wirt had expressed many times in his writings.[13]

But character and tradition were no longer sufficient recommendations for high political office in the rough-and-tumble political climate of the 1830s. Neither Wirt nor Clay summoned enough support to unseat Old Hickory. Jackson took 219 out of 286 electoral votes. Wirt won only Vermont, with its seven votes in the electoral college. In fairness, Wirt's popularity in that state had as much to do with his valiant defense of Vermont native Worcester, the missionary to the Cherokees, as the Anti-Masonic drawing power. Wirt also showed remarkable strength in Pennsylvania, capturing 40 percent of the popular vote. Clay did not fare much better, with 49 electoral votes, winning Connecticut, Rhode Island, Massachusetts, Delaware, Maryland and Kentucky. The election of 1832 went down in the history books as another Jackson landslide. In popular vote it was closer. Jackson polled 661,000 votes, Clay 300,000, Wirt 100,000; and in New York, a combined Clay-Wirt ticket received 154,000 votes.[14] Two years later, John Quincy Adams would observe about Wirt's reluctant candidacy: "a very little difference in the state of the public mind at that time would have effected his election as president of the United States."[15]

The Anti-Masonic movement did not die out completely with the election of 1832. In the wake of Jackson's victory, the *Providence American* put Wirt's name forward as a likely Presidential candidate in 1836. When Wirt read this article which was reprinted in many papers, he quickly set his would-be supporters straight. "I consider the nomination which I accepted as being finally disposed of by the recent election... I take no pleasure, but the reverse, in seeing my name the renewed subject of newspaper discussion for a purpose so remote and so contingent."[16]

Chapter 23

The Clock Winds Down

The strain of work and his lifelong quest for "the good life" began to take its toll on Wirt as he passed the half-century mark. Work kept him at the office until "nine or ten at night, when I come home, take my tea, talk over family affairs, and get to bed between eleven and twelve," he complained in a letter to the Rev. John H. Rice on February 1, 1822. "But it is killing me; and as death would be extremely inconvenient to me, in more respects than one, at this time, I shall quit that course of operations and look a little to my health, if I can survive the approaching Supreme Court... I am sick of public life. My skin is too thin for the business. A politician should have the hide of a rhinoceros."[1]

Alas, that term of the Supreme Court almost did Wirt in. At its close, he was nearly incapacitated by a fever, brought on by the heavy public and private workload he insisted on carrying. Wirt survived to carry on, but his great foe Pinkney was not so fortunate. He died on February 25, 1822, while arguing a case. On May 9, a convalescing Wirt wrote Francis Gilmer: "I keep my mind void of care – read novels, ride, walk, play at battledore, and take as much exercise as I can bear. Tazewell, and Webster, meantime, have been reaping laurels in the Supreme Court, and I have been – sighing. Poor Pinkney! He died opportunely for his fame. It could not have risen higher... He was a great man. On a set occasion, the greatest, I think, at our bar... Poor Pinkney! After all, how long will he be remembered? He has left no monument of his genius behind him, and posterity will, therefore, know nothing of such a man but by the report of others."[2]

Wirt had a few good years left, however, and seemed to shared, with Madison and other contemporaries, somewhat of a preoccupation with personal health that bordered on hypochondria. Like today, health worries made a good topic of conversation. Wirt's many letters to friends made frequent reference to his state of mind and physical condition. And because of his prolific pen and the state of preservation of this correspondence, those who study them are more cognizant of Wirt's health than they would be with a more reticent historical figure.

Still, there is little doubt that Wirt's lifestyle had a ravaging effect on his body. Wirt's marriage to Betsy Gamble toned down an unbridled lifestyle of wine, women and song. But Wirt never achieved total abstinence until it became a medical necessity later in life and constantly struggled to maintain what anyone would call a harmonious state of moderation. He remained fond of snuff, cigars and good wine. In his home, Wirt kept generous supplies of whiskey and wine. He was particularly fond of Sicilian vintages and complained that they were not always available in the marketplaces of Richmond and the District of Columbia. A good wife, Betsy did her best to curb her husband's appetites, but it was an uphill struggle, at best. She was known to complain that at some gatherings in their home, she could barely see Wirt's friends "through the vapor of the grape and smoke of cigars." Wirt spoke easily about inviting 21 gentlemen over for venison and admitted that his wife had a tendency to become "uneasy" that his guests might tempt him into "frolics." As might be expected, the food and drink gathered about Wirt's waistline. In 1817, he wrote Dabney Carr, saying he was "hearty as a buck" and "fat as a fool."[3]

In the early 1800s, medicine was an inexact science and there was a great deal of truth in the expression, "the cure was worse than the illness." Professor Robert noted that Wirt once attempted to cure a toothache by extracting the tooth on his own. When the tooth snapped off even with the jaw, Wirt treated the pain with one of "his favorite remedies, calomel and julep, and cupped blood from both arms – from all of which he luckily recovered. Later in life, Wirt "enjoyed the luxury of washing his head in whiskey, a practice which must have given him a sensational aroma when he appeared before the courts," Robert also noted.[4]

In 1831, Wirt's health took another turn for the worse, no doubt exacerbated by the untimely death of his youngest daughter, Agnes, 16, to whom he was particularly close. Wirt was heartbroken by this event and never fully recovered. "She was my companion, my office companion, my librarian, my clerk," he wrote. "She pursued her studies in my office, by my side – sat with me, walked with me, was my inexpressibly sweet and inseparable companion – never left me but to go sit with her mother. We knew all her intelligence, all her pure and delicate sensibility, the quickness and power of her perceptions, her seraphic love. She was all love, and loved all God's creation, even the animals, trees and plants. She loved her God and Savior with an angel's love and died like a saint." Wirt was noticeably depressed for an extended period after his daughter's death and began to deteriorate physically. At the time of Agnes' death, Wirt was embroiled in the impeachment trial of Judge Peck. The Senate adjourned the trial for a week. But for several weeks afterward, Wirt relied on his co-counsel to keep things moving. It was fully a month later before Wirt was able to make his impassioned speech in Peck's defense, and that "under the pressure of ill-health and deep affliction of spirit."[5]

On March 8, 1833, Wirt wrote his son-in-law Judge Randall, "My health has been much better this winter than for several winters past. I am not much more than half the size I was at forty. My spirits, though not boisterous, as once they were, are good and almost buoyant. *The blow struck on my heart, two winters ago, I shall never get over; nor can I say I wish to get over it...* I am, indeed, often surprised at my own cheerfulness, and sometimes, a little ashamed of my levity. If I were in Florida I might be as undignified as I please, without censure, save from myself. [6]

Because of the threat of warm–weather illnesses and fevers in the lowlands the Wirts often summered in the mountains and at the mineral springs of Virginia. Wirt would spend as much time there with his family as possible, commuting to the courts of Richmond, Washington, and Baltimore. Much of his later correspondence is dated Montevideo, White Sulphur Springs and Red Sulphur Springs.

In August, 1833, Wirt wrote to one of his law students, S. Treackle Wallis, from Red Sulphur Springs, "the remotest of the mineral waters of Virginia," saying he expected to tarry there until October – "these waters agree with me marvelously well so far. According to the report of scales, I am gaining a pound here every day – and am sensible of great improvement in my strength, good feelings and appetite."[7]

Wirt's health continued to rebound through Christmas, 1833. "Merrier Christmases we have both seen, than, I suppose, we shall ever see again.. But cheerful Christmases we may still have, for our hearts have not yet grown cold," he wrote to his old friend Judge Carr. "I am rattling among the dry bones of my records for the Supreme Court. We go down on the 11th of next month. My health is so good that I hope to be able to bear all the labors of the winter without flinching, and to meet you at Lewisburg next summer, in better plight than I did last."[8]

To his brother-in-law, Judge Cabell, Wirt wrote of Christmases past: "I said to Mrs. W. just now, 'let us send for Dr. H. and Cabell to help us make egg-nog for our company. Poor, dear H.!... I think I can see him now, every moment hear his voice, see his dry, funny smile, and smack of his lips on tasting the egg-nog."[9]

He wrote his oldest daughter Laura and son-in-law, Judge Randall, in Florida that he hoped to move there by 1835. "I am in good health, now, thank Heaven! But quite lean. The rest of us are well." But the next mail from Florida brought sad tidings. Laura Wirt Randall had died of pulmonary disease on December 17, 1833. Wirt had lost a second daughter in less than three years. In relaying this news to his friend Cabell, Wirt wrote, philosophically about death: "I look upon life as a drama, bearing the same sort, though not the same degree of relation to eternity, as an hour spent at the theatre and the fictions there exhibited for our instruction, do to the whole of real life... Now, when my children or friends leave me, or when I shall be called to leave them, I consider it as merely parting for the present visit, to meet under happier circumstances when we shall part no more."[10]

Chapter 24

The Florida Fling

Although the law was the only investment Wirt made that ever paid off, he fancied himself an entrepreneur, investing his hard-won legal fees in a number of schemes. Unfortunately, his various failed business ventures only forced him to work harder as a lawyer.

Wirt's part ownership in the Bellona Foundry, a cannon factory on Spring Creek near Richmond, seemed a sound investment in the wake of the War of 1812. His partner was Major John Clarke, the deposed state superintendent of arms manufactory. Despite an agreement by the government to buy 300 tons of cannon in 1815, the venture never made the partners wealthy. Quality control seemed to be a problem. Seven of Clarke's cannon exploded when test fired by ordinance inspectors in 1833, one fragment crashing into a wall of the adjacent Bellona Arsenal. Location was also a problem. The level of water in Spring Creek was often insufficient to drive the machinery. The arsenal's repair shops were relocated to Fort Monroe in 1832 and the arsenal was later leased to Thomas Mann Randolph, who tried to cultivate silk worms there. In 1856, Secretary of War Jefferson Davis sold the arsenal for $2,650 to Clarke's grandson, Dr. Junius L. Archer, who had inherited the foundry. Five years later, Clarke put the foundry and arsenal at the disposal of the Confederacy, but it was never much of a factor in the war effort.[1] Wirt's investment in the foundry became something of a political liability when he became Attorney General. Monroe saw no conflict of interest in his Attorney General having ownership in a defense contractor, however, so Wirt did not terminate the arrangement. With his love for classical literature, Wirt undoubtedly had a hand in naming the foundry. *Bellona* was the Roman goddess of war.

In the twilight of his life, Wirt became embroiled in another financial catastrophe. On the advice of his son-in-law, Navy Lieutenant Louis Goldsborough, Wirt set about creating a colony of 150 German immigrants on land he bought in the Florida

Territory. Thomas Randall, who married Wirt's eldest daughter Laura, was appointed a District Judge in Tallahassee in 1827, undoubtedly through the influence of his proud father-in-law. The Randalls and Wirt's brothers-in-law Robert and John Gamble bought plantations just east of Tallahassee. Eyeing Florida as a place to retire where he could live graciously surrounded by family, Wirt bought large parcels of land in Jackson, Gadsden, Leon and Jefferson counties while he was still Attorney General. Wirt had special interest in a 1,200-acre tract of pine land at the south end of Lake Miccosukee, where he intended to grow sugar cane, and a second tract four miles southwest of Monticello, the county seat of Jefferson County. Because of the difficulty in finding African slaves in western Florida, many of the Virginians settling there brought slaves with them. The Gamble brothers, who borrowed heavily from relatives and Virginia banks to finance their venture, were hard hit by the early freeze in 1831. Their capacity for producing crystal sugar was destroyed, but they were able to salvage part of their crop to make rum and molasses.[2]

Wirt pondered the economic potential of his land purchases for several years before making a move. In 1833, Wirt and Goldsborough hatched a scheme to work the land with immigrant German "partners" as an alternative to African slaves. Wirt wrote Judge Randall to announce the plan and ask for his assistance: "If the project succeeds there will be a safe and ready and peaceful refuge for my family in the event of my death. If I could live to see them comfortably established on their own lands in Florida, life would go out with me as sweetly as a babe sleeps." Recalling his own German-Swiss heritage, Wirt watched with interest the many German immigrants coming through the Port of Baltimore. On January 29, he wrote Randall: "There are many Germans of sober and industrious habits, walking on the Avenue here. They have their wives and children. Many of them are mechanics, carpenters, mill-wrights, bricklayers, &c. How would it do to send a hundred and fifty of these people out, under Louis Goldsborough, to work my lands on shares?" Goldsborough, then 28, persuaded Wirt to set the colony up along the lines of a whaling ship. "The only pay the sailor gets in these voyages," Wirt explained to his wife, is what they call a *lay* – that is, a share of the profits. And yet they are the happiest and most faithful of seamen... I offer to take them out at my own expense, support them till the plantation will maintain them... and to give them one-third of the clear profits... They will form a fine little village in the settlement, with their gardens in the rear of the dwellings, a broad street between, and a church, schoolhouse and parsonage at one end... The project is new in our country – looks rather visionary, and very like one of the castles in the air; but practical men here think it must succeed."[3]

Another German-American, Congressman Henry A. Muhlenberg of Pennsylvania, encouraged Wirt in his endeavor, saying he was astonished Virginians hadn't struck on such a scheme as an alternative to slavery. He did, however, bring up two possible problems, the climate and the ignorance of the immigrants about the cultivation of sugar and cotton. Florida's territorial Governor also endorsed Wirt's plan to clear the land and populate it with immigrants. "If the Germans continue faithful, it is, he admits, a great and splendid enterprise. He says it is a fine country for silk, with plenty of white mulberries; fine too, for vines; and he recommends your carrying out a plenty of slips of the grape vine of all kinds," Wirt wrote Goldsborough. A doting parent, Wirt insulated his son-in-law against the possibility of failure. "Don't suffer this enterprise to weigh too heavily on your mind. We all know that you will do your best... Every human project depends on so many thousand contingencies, against which no thought, sagacity or prudence can guard, that no man or woman of sense is surprised at the failure of anything."[4]

Wirt and his son-in-law encountered numerous difficulties in obtaining reliable transportation and the requisite number of Germans for their admittedly risky venture. But on March 22, Wirt announced the departure of the *Laurel* with Goldsborough and 150 Germans on board. To ensure a homogeneous group, they were all Protestants and all from Bavaria or the surrounding countryside, and they were accompanied by their pastor, who would also serve as schoolmaster for the children. Wirt made sure to include a supply of German primers, Psalters, slates, pencils and "coarse writing paper for their copybooks." They sailed, Wirt said, "with a fine smacking breeze from the west." The colonists, he noted, seemed "greatly attached" to Goldsborough. "A truer, nobler, kinder, braver fellow never lived. I never doubted the *lion* part of his composition, but I never saw so much of the *lamb*, till within the last few days."[5]

Undoubtedly remembering his brother and cousin, who sailed out of the Chesapeake Bay some 50 years before and never were heard from again, Wirt fretted about the safety of his son-in-law and his charges. In a letter postmarked eight days after the *Laurel* sailed, Wirt wrote to Goldsborough: "Your argosy, is so richly freighted with human lives, that we shall be exceedingly solicitous till we hear of your being on *terra firma* again. When I learn you have got your colony in Wirtland, and that your Germans are busily and cheerfully engaged in building their village, I shall feel greatly relieved and comparatively secure. Every cabin, with its garden and milch cow, will be a new anchor to windward... The predictions are generally unfavorable to your success, but it is by those who do not understand your plan, and judge of it by the general conduct of German redemptioners only. Ours are not redemptioners, but partners in trade; and I argue more favorably of the result."[6]

After a rough time at sea and a longer voyage than anticipated, Wirt's colonists landed in Florida in late April. "What a time you have had of it? Six days on the Grand Bank near the Hole in the Wall! – and you all came safe ashore, except the poor little canary bird which [Elizabeth] takes it for granted is now warbling away, and 'dancing canary' in the West Indies. We are all delighted with your care and attention to the Germans, and their civility, contentment and good behavior throughout the voyage. I begin to feel increasing confidence in their adherence to you," Wirt wrote Goldsborough on April 30.[7]

An experienced seaman, Wirt's son-in-law may have been guilty of romanticizing the journey. Goldsborough's early accounts of the voyage and the high morale among the band of sea-sick Germans who staggered ashore only to be greeted by untamed wilderness and an unfamiliar climate did not prepare Wirt for the early collapse of their colonization effort. Within two months, the bulk of the settlers had hightailed it out of Wirtland in search of greener pastures. When he received word in July, while taking the healthful waters of White Sulphur Springs, Virginia, Wirt wrote Goldsborough a consoling note: "With regard to the Germans, considering what kind of cattle they have proved to be, I am so far from lamenting their desertion, that I think it quite a happy riddance... Never mind the affair. It is only one of 'our castles' tumbled down. I am so used to such things that I am rather more disposed to laugh than to weep at them. Thank heaven, there are no bones broke in the way of pecuniary loss! We had, at least, the foresight to anticipate such a result, and to take care to make the experiment as cheaply as possible. I am sorry for your disappointment. But regrets are vain. The thing has been done. We must not be unnerved by the disappointment, but provide as vigorously as we can to meet the future... Good wishes to the Messrs. Mohl and all the faithful among the Germans."[8]

There is an indication that Wirt's Germans received considerable persuasion to abandon the venture. Judge Randall wrote Wirt about "the active mischief of some bad and designing people here." The Germans, he added, had been physically assaulted and intimidated by local ruffians stirred up by rumors that the colonists were part of a plot to upset the political balance in the area. "These ignorant people," Randall explained, thought Goldsborough would control the votes of the German colonists, should they stay on. When Wirt replied that he had his fill of the "Banditti Society" of Florida, Randall urged him not to judge Jefferson County by the "offenses of a few Georgia Crackers."[9]

To Randall, Wirt wrote: "I wonder how Louis has been able to bear up under it. I am infinitely more sorry on his account than my own... I have read in some book 'that life is nothing more than a succession of bloated hopes and withering disappointments.' The expression is somewhat too strong, for there is certainly some present enjoyment in life. I have had my share of it... Indeed, the explosion has been so quick and so complete, and there is something so droll in those rascals having gone so far to play so ridiculous a caper, that it seems to me rather more laughable than cryable."[10]

The colonial caper cost Wirt about $8,000, no small sum in 1833, but it did not prove a major setback for either Wirt or Goldsborough. Wirt was sufficiently well off that he could chuckle over his losses. His son-in-law continued his Navy service. Goldsborough saw action in the Mexican War, explored the coast of California and Oregon in 1849-50, and was Superintendent of the U.S. Naval Academy from 1853-57. During the Civil War, Goldsborough remained loyal to the Union. He commanded the flotilla that captured Roanoke Island and destroyed the Confederate Fleet in 1862. Goldsborough retired as a Rear Admiral.[11]

Wirt was persuaded by Randall to cultivate his Miccosukee Plantation by the more conventional method of using African slaves. Forty slaves were purchased from Achille Murat at an average price of $275 apiece. Randall's friend Pope Hunter had been overseer of Murat's slaves and knew them to be reliable.[12] One of the more colorful inhabitants of the Florida Territory, Murat was the eldest son of Napoleon's youngest sister, Caroline, and Joachim Murat, a cavalryman who served both Louis XVI and Bonaparte. Under his brother-in-law's tutelage,

Joachim Murat became Governor of the Cisalpine Republic and the City of Paris, Marshal and Grand Admiral of the Empire, and King of Naples. When he was five, Achille Murat was named Duke of the Rhine Provinces of Berg and Cleves. At seven, Achille became the Crown Prince of Naples, which allowed him to escape Napoleon's unpleasant habit of pulling his nephew's ears. By 1823, however, Achille Murat was an exile cast upon America's shores. After sampling New Jersey, the District of Columbia and St. Augustine, he settled in Tallahassee, where, in 1826, he married Catherine Daingerfield Gray, a 23-year-old widow and great-grand niece of George Washington. Murat was soon off on new adventures in Europe, Louisiana and Texas, however, and his bank loans became overdue, necessitating the sale of slaves to Wirt.[13]

Although he would not live to take up residence in Florida, Wirt's Florida holdings flourished under the supervision of Randall and Goldsborough. By 1835, a screw press capable of bailing 8,000 pounds of cotton a day had been installed there. In the same year, a mansion was built at Wirtland. Wirt's widow and children spent a good bit of time there after his death. When Goldsborough went back to sea in 1839, William Wirt's son, Dabney Carr Wirt, managed the plantation while studying law. Wirt's son-in-law, Thomas Randall, served as a superior court judge for 12 years, but always considered himself first a planter. The Gamble brothers also prospered in West Florida after mastering the initial hardships.[14]

Chapter 25

The End

William Wirt went to Washington D.C. in good spirits for the January, 1834, term of the Supreme Court. He had several important cases there and attended court regularly. On Saturday evening, February 8, he told a friend that he was in good spirits and confident of the argument he would make before the high court on Monday. On Sunday, he walked a mile from his boarding house to attend church services at the Capitol. It was a cold, damp day and the Representatives' Hall was hot and stuffy. On Monday he complained of a cold and sent for a doctor. The "cold" developed into another bout of erysipelas.[1] Wirt's health deteriorated all week. On Saturday he lost consciousness, despite the ministrations of two physicians, who placed hot bricks around his body, applied scalding poultices to his feet and placed 40 leeches on his left temple and left ear. Wirt argued old cases in his delirium. On Monday, he briefly regained consciousness and was surrounded by family and a clergyman. When Wirt heard the prayers for his recovery, he moaned, "No... No!" William Wirt died at 11 a.m., Tuesday, February 18, 1834.[2]

After receiving word, the Supreme Court immediately adjourned for the day. On the 19th, the members of the bar gathered in the courtroom. In a session chaired by Attorney General Benjamin F. Butler, Daniel Webster paid tribute to Wirt:

"It is announced to us that one of the oldest, one of the ablest, one of the most distinguished members of this Bar, has departed this mortal life. William Wirt is no more! He has this day closed a professional career among the longest and most brilliant, which the distinguished members of the profession in the United States have at any time accomplished. Unsullied in everything which regards professional honor and integrity, patient of labor, and rich in those stores of learning, which are the reward of patient labor and patient labor only; and if equaled, yet certainly allowed not to be excelled, in fervent, animated and persuasive eloquence, he has left an example, which those who seek to raise themselves to great heights of professional eminence, will hereafter emulously [sic] study. Fortunate, indeed, will be the few who shall imitate it successfully![3]

"As a public man, it is not our peculiar duty to speak of Mr. Wirt here. His character, in that respect, belongs to his country, and to the history of his country. And, sir, if we were to speak of him in his private life and in his social relations, all we could possibly say of his urbanity, his kindness, the faithfulness of his friendships, and the warmth of his affections, would hardly seem sufficiently strong and glowing to do him justice, in the feeling and judgment of those who, separated now forever from his embraces, can only enshrine his memory in their bleeding hearts ...But our particular ties to him were the ties of our profession. He was our brother and he was our friend. With talents, powerful enough to excite the strength of the strongest, with a kindness of heart and of manner capable of warming and winning the coldest of his brethren, he has now completed the term of his professional life and of his earthly existence, in the enjoyment of the high respect and cordial affections of us all. Let us then, sir, hasten to pay to his memory the well deserved tribute of our regard. Let us lose no time in testifying our sense of our loss and in expressing our grief, that one great light of our profession is extinguished forever."[4]

A committee was appointed to see to Wirt's burial in the Congressional Cemetery in Washington D.C., and to erect an obelisk to his memory. To this request, Chief Justice Marshall replied, "I am sure I utter the sentiment of all my brethren when I say we participate sincerely in the feelings expressed from the Bar. We, too, gentlemen, have sustained a loss it will be difficult, if not impossible to repair. In performing the arduous duties assigned us, we have been long aided by the diligent research and lucid reasoning of him whose loss we unite with you in deploring."[5]

Wirt was buried on February 20, 1834. The Senate and the House of Representatives adjourned so members could attend the funeral. President Andrew Jackson, Vice President Martin Van Buren, ex-President Adams, and Chief Justice Marshall walked in the funeral procession. They were joined by many others, including Henry Clay, John Calhoun, Daniel Webster, Maj. Gen. Winfield Scott, General of the Army Alexander Macomb, Navy Commissioner Isaac Chauncey, Secretary of the Navy Levi Woodbury, Justice Joseph Story, Senator Samuel

Southard, Secretary of the Treasury Roger B. Taney, Secretary of War Lewis Cass, and Congressmen Horace Binney and Edward Everett.[6]

On the day after Wirt's burial, John Quincy Adams addressed the House of Representatives:

"Mr. Wirt had never been a member of either House of Congress. But if his form in marble, or his portrait upon canvass were placed within these walls, a suitable inscription for it would be that of the statue of Moliere in the Hall of the French Academy – 'Nothing was wanting to *his* glory: *He* was wanting to ours.' – For a period of twelve years, during two successive administrations of the National Government, he had been the official and confidential adviser, upon all questions of law, of the Presidents of the United States; and he had discharged the duties of that station entirely to the satisfaction of those officers and of the country... nor risk I contradiction in affirming that they were never more ably or more faithfully discharged than by Mr. Wirt.

"If a mind stored with all the learning appropriate to the profession of the law, and decorated with all the elegance of classical literature; if a spirit imbued with the sensibilities of a lofty patriotism, and chastened by the meditations of a profound philosophy – if a brilliant imagination, a discerning intellect, a sound judgment, an indefatigable capacity, and vigorous energy of application, vivified with an ease and rapidity of elocution, copious without redundance, and select without affectation – if all of these, united with a sportive vein of humor, an inoffensive temper, and an angelic purity of heart – if all of these in their combination are the qualities suitable for an Attorney General of the United States – in him, they were all eminently combined...

"But it is not my purpose to pronounce his eulogy. That pleasing task has been assigned to abler hands, and to a more suitable occasion. He will there be presented in other, though not less interesting lights. As the penetrating delineator of manners and character in the British Spy – as the biographer of Patrick Henry, dedicated to the young men of your native commonwealth – as the friend and delight of the social circle – as the husband and father in the bosom of a happy, but now most afflicted family – in all these characters I have known, admired and loved him..." Adams said.[7]

Judges and lawyers in many states also held gatherings to pay tribute to Wirt. His obituary received prominent treatment in many of the newspapers of the land. The *American Beacon* of Norfolk reported on February 22, 1934:

"We noticed very briefly, yesterday, the painful intelligence brought by the Steam Boat Columbia, the death of William Wirt, Esq., a gentleman who had few equals in our land, in whose endowments of mind and person, which constitutes an eminent citizen. Mr. Wirt was alike distinguished for the extent and profundity of his legal learning, his brilliant attainments in solid and ornamental literature, his transcendent oratorical powers, his public services as Attorney General of the Republic, and his civic and domestic virtues – it may be most appropriately said of him, that no man in our country mingled more felicitously, the useful with the attractive and endearing qualification for the highest walks of life. ... The universal affection and respect in which this rarely endowed citizen was held in this state and this town especially, where he resided for several years after he resigned the Chancellorship of the Williamsburg District, has called for something more, at our hands, than a passing record of the fact that, *a great man has fallen in our land!* It is no less due to these considerations that we spread upon our columns the following just and affecting testimonials of the high regard in which he was held..." This localized obituary was followed by a reprint of an obituary that first appeared in the *National Intelligencer* on February 19, as well as a reprint of Webster's remarks to the Supreme Court.[8]

Although Wirt is not a household name today, his fame did not die with him. For many years after his death, William Wirt Societies and "Literary Institutes" flourished in many eastern cities dedicated to excellence in oratory and literature. Edgar Allan Poe, who had once gone to Wirt for advice, spoke at one of them.[9] Wirt County, Virginia (now West Virginia) was created in 1848 and named after the late Attorney General. Whigs were prominent in the political scene of Wood County, from which Wirt county was split off. William Wirt was still very much alive in their memories, 14 years after his death. [10]

George W. Sherwood presented a eulogy on Wirt to the Baltimore William Wirt Society on October 22, 1834. "His unassuming manners and frankness made him a man to be honored, as he was; revered as he is; and though he has carried to the tomb an unblemished name, as a public man, he has left behind him an increasing love in the hearts of those who better know his private worth," Sherwood said. "Indeed, the young, the old and aged _ the mighty and the powerless, the abject and forlorn, will find a balmy moral in the life of Mr. Wirt, in which we see the apparent insurmountable obstacles of life all overleaped with bounding majesty, by industry and perseverance." [11]

William Wirt was so successful and likable that he inspired emulation, both during his lifetime and after. John Pendleton Kennedy patterned his life after Wirt and, in 1849 published a thorough, but ponderous 867-page, two volume, *Memoirs of the Life of William Wirt, Attorney General of the United States.* Somewhat inaccurate and gushingly complimentary, Kennedy's *Memoirs of Wirt* preserved many of Wirt's speeches, courtroom arguments, letters and anecdotes. Collections of Wirt's letters and papers can be found at the Maryland Historical Society (more than 8,000 items available on microfilm), the Library of Congress, the National Archives, The Virginia State Library and Archives, the Virginia Historical Society, the Alderman Library at the University of Virginia, the Swem Library at the College of William & Mary and other institutions. Because he was so prolific, much more remains on paper of Wirt's life than that of many other prominent men of the nation's first half-century.

On the anniversary of Wirt's birth in 1972, Dr. Joseph C. Robert, who served as President of Hampden-Sydney College, President of the Virginia Historical Society, and later the William Binford Vest Professor of History at the University of Richmond, took note of the inattention paid to the man who was the confidant of four presidents, a distinguished lawyer, writer and orator, and the longest-serving Attorney General in the country's history. "...Wirt is scarcely mentioned in our textbooks. And when he is remembered too often it is only to be classified inferentially as an eccentric, if not worse, for accepting the Anti-Masonic nomination, or to be criticized for his eulogistic *Sketches of the Life and Character of Patrick Henry.* Graduate Students are told to 'de-Wirt' their seminar reports! As for Wirt, the gap between the man's prestige during his lifetime and now is greater than for any other public figure in American history."[12]

Notes on Chapters 1-25

Chapter 1: A Life of Accomplishment

1. John Pendleton Kennedy, Memoirs of the Life of William Wirt, Attorney General of the United States, vol. II, Lea and Blanchard (Philadelphia, 1849), reprinted in 1973 as *Classics in Legal History*, vols. 19-20, p. 425-427. Hereafter cited as Kennedy I or II.
2. Kennedy II, p. 214-215.
3. Richard Beale Davis, *Intellectual Life in Jefferson's Virginia, 1790-1830*, University of North Carolina Press (Chapel Hill, 1964), 2nd printing by University of Tennessee Press (1972), 385 Hereafter cited as Davis. (footnote on page 475 identifies locations in New Jersey, Philadelphia and Western Pennsylvania.).

Chapter 2: A Promising Youth

1. Peter Hoffman Cruse, "Biographical Sketch of William Wirt," introduction to William Wirt, The Letters of the British Spy, 10th edition, (New York, 1832), p. 11. Hereafter cited as Cruse.
2. John Pendleton Kennedy, *Memoirs of the Life of William Wirt, Attorney General of the United States*, vol. I, p. 16. Hereafter cited as Kennedy I.
3. Robert, "William Wirt, Virginian," *Virginia Magazine of History & Biography*, Vol. 80, No. 4 (October, 1972), p. 389. Hereafter known as Robert WWV.
4. Kennedy I, p. 27.
5. *Ibid.* p. 27-28.
6. *Ibid.*, p. 19-22.
7. Cruse, p. 12-13.
8. *Ibid.*, p. 22-23.
10. *Ibid.*, p. 26.
11. Cruse, p. 15-16.
11. *Ibid.*, 15-16.
12. Kennedy I, p. 29.
13. *Ibid.*, p. 30.
14. *Ibid.*, p. 31.
15. *Ibid*, p. 32-36.
16. *Ibid*, p. 37-39.
17. *Ibid*, page 47-48.
18. Robert WWV, p. 393-4.
19. Cruse, p. 29-32.
20. W. Wirt to William Pope, Dec. 14, 1828, quoted in Robert WWV, p. 394.
21. W. Wirt to Peter Carnes, William Wirt Papers, Maryland Historical Society, Microfilm reel 1. (Also quoted in Kennedy I.)

Chapter 3: Established in Virginia

1. Wirt to Peter Carnes, Nov. 1792, Wirt Papers, Maryland Historical Society, Baltimore, Microfilm Reel 1.
2. Cruse, p. 35-39.
3. Kennedy I p. 60-61.
4. Rev. P. Slaughter, *Memoir of Col. Joshua Fry with an Autobiography of his Son, Rev. Henry Fry,* date unknown. (publication courtesy of Fry descendant Mrs. William Wetsel, Locust Dale, Virginia.)
5. *Ibid.*

6.Francis Taylor, *Diary of Col. Francis Taylor*, (Orange County, Va., 1786-1799) Library of Virginia Archives and Records Division.)
7. Madison County Court Records, 1793, Madison, Virginia.
8. Cruse, p. 36.
9. Kennedy I, p. 61.
10. 1795 Defense of Marshall & Patterson, Wirt Papers, Maryland Historical Society, quoted in Robert, WWV, p. 396.
11. Kennedy I, p. 64-67.
12. Gilmer Family File, Albemarle County Historical Society, Charlottesville.
13. Kennedy I, p. 63-73.

Chapter 4: Useful Alliances Forged
1. Kennedy I, p. 63-73.
2. Cruse, p. 35-39.
3. Wirt to Dabney Carr, Spring, 1799, quoted in Kennedy, p. 72.
4. Kennedy I, p. 69-72.
5. *Ibid.*
6. Robert, WWV, p. 397.
7. Taylor Diary.
8. Kennedy I, p. 66-68.
9. Kennedy I, p. 75-76.

Chapter 5: A Change of Venue
1. Kennedy I, p. 76-78 and Robert, WWV, p. 398-399.
2. *Ibid.*, p. 78-79.
3. *Ibid.*, p. 80-86.
4. *Ibid.*
5. Virginius Dabney, *The Jefferson Scandals, A Rebuttal*, (New York, 1981), p. 6-15.
6. Statement by Judge Chase, quoted in Kennedy I, p. 85.
7. Kennedy I, p. 79-80.
8. Kenendy I, p. 91-92.
9. Gov. James Monroe to Wirt, February, 1802, quoted in Kennedy I, p. 88-89.
10. Wirt to Dabney Carr, February 12, 1802, quoted in Kennedy I, p. 89.
11. Wirt to Col. Gamble, Wirt Papers, Reel 1.
12. Wirt to Dabney Carr, Feb. 13, 1803, quoted in Kennedy I, p. 94-95.
13. Wirt Folder, Archives of the College of William & Mary, Williamsburg.

Chapter 6: Private Practice Resumed
1. Wirt to Dabney Carr, March 20, 1803, quoted in Kennedy I, p. 96-98.
2. Wirt to Carr, June 6, 1803, cited in Kennedy I, p. 99-100.
3. Wirt. to William Pope, August 5, 1803, quoted in Kennedy I, p. 102-104.
4. *Ibid.*
5. Wirt to Elizabeth Wirt, (undated), quoted in Kennedy I, p. 104-108.
6. *Ibid.*
7. *Ibid*, p. 106-108.
8. Thomas Wertenbacher, *Norfolk: Historic Southern Port*, (Durham, 1931) p. 140-145. Hereafter referred to as *Norfolk*.
9. Kennedy I, p. 118-123.
10. La Rochefoucauld-Liancourt, Francois A, Duc de, *Voyages darrs les Etats-Unis*, vol. IV, p. 256-257, quoted in *Norfolk*, p. 141.
11. Norfolk *Herald*, July 18, 1803.

12. William Couper, *Letters of William Couper*, August 19, 1802, quoted in *Norfolk*, p. 140.
13. Thomas Moore, Norfolk *Gazette and Public Ledger*, Sept. 12, 1806, quoted in *Norfolk*, p. 141.
14. Wirt to Benj. Edwards, March 17, 1805, quoted in Kennedy I, p. 132-139.
15. Kennedy I, p. 136.
16. Elizabeth Wirt to Wirt, August 4, 1805, *Wirt Papers* MHS, quoted in Robert, Robert, *WWV*, p. 410
17. Kennedy I, p. 142, 148.
18. Norfolk *Public Ledger,* August 8, 1806. Microfilm in Kirn Memorial Library, Norfolk, Va.

Chapter 7: The 'British Spy'

1. Wirt to Carr, January 16, 1804, cited in Kennedy I, p. 111-115.
2. William Wirt, *The Letters of the British Spy*, 10th Edition, Harper & Brothers, (New York, 1832), p. 207-208. Hereafter cited as Wirt, *Spy*.
3. Wirt to Carr, January 16, 1804, quoted in Kennedy I, p. 111-123.
4. Wirt, *Spy*, p. 173-176.
5. *Ibid.*, p. 106-107.
6. *Ibid.*, p. 161-165.
7. *Ibid.*, p. 196-201.
8. Jay Hubbell, *The South in American Literature*, p. 241, quoted in William R. Taylor, "William Wirt and the Legend of the Old South," *William & Mary Quarterly, series 3, vol. 14, No. 4, p. 484.*
9. William R. Taylor, *Cavalier and Yankee; the Old South and American National Character,* (New York, 1961), p. 67-94, hereafter known as Taylor, *Cavalier.*
10. Wirt to Benjamin Edwards, March 17, 1805, quoted in Kennedy I, p. 133-139. (This letter is signed affectionately, "Your son by election, Wm. Wirt.")

Chapter 8: George Wythe Murder Case

1. Wirt to Elizabeth Wirt, quoted in Kennedy, p. 151-154.
2. Statement by Thomas Jefferson, quoted in Julian P. Boyd & Edwin Hemphill, *The Murder of George Wythe, Two Essays.* The Insitute of Early American History and Culture, (Williamsburg, 1955). p. 1-18. Hereafter cited as Boyd & Hemphill.
3. Wirt to James Monroe, June 10, 1806, Monroe Papers, Vol. XI, No. 1373, Library of Congress, quoted in Boyd & Hemphill.
4. Boyd & Hemphill, p. 1-58.
5. *Ibid.*
6. *Ibid.*
7. *Ibid.*
8. Edwin Hemphill, "Documents on the Murder of George Wythe," *William and Mary Quarterly*, Third Series, Vol. XII, October, 1995, p. 551-560.
9. *Ibid*, p. 560-562. Hereafter cited as Hemphill.
10. Boyd & Hemphill, p. 29-31.
11 Hemphill, p. 569-572.
12. *Ibid.*, p. 569-573.
13. Wirt to Elizabeth Wirt (undated), quoted in Kennedy I, p. 140.

Chapter 9: The Burr Treason Trial

1. Kennedy I, p. 163-166.
2. Washington Irving, quoted in S. H. Wandell & Meade Minnigerode, *Aaron Burr*, v. II, (New York, 1925), p. 184-197. Hereafter cited as *Burr*.
3. Washington Irving, quoted in *Burr*, p. 199.
4. Robert, *WWV*, p. 412.
5. Washington Irving, quoted in *Burr*, p. 194-199.
6. *Burr*, p. 185, 202-203.
7. Kennedy I, p. 185-195.
8. Davis, p. 384.
9. Kennedy I, p. 206.
10. Burr, p. 215-217.
11. Wirt to Dabney Carr, September 1, 1807, quoted in Kennedy I, p. 220-221.
12. Burr, p. 219-220.
13. Davis, p. 384.
14. Unpublished letter from Wirt to Dabney Carr, cited in Robert, Hon. Wirt, p. 57, and in Taylor, *Cavalier*, p. 76.

Chapter 10: Political Arena Beckons

1. Wirt to Dabney Carr, July 2, 1807, quoted in Kennedy I, p. 207-216.
2. Wirt to Carr, July 28, 1807, quoted in Kennedy, p. 217-225.
3. Thomas Jefferson to Wirt, January 10, 1808, in Kennedy I, p. 227-228.
4. Wirt to Thomas Jefferson, January 14, 1808, in Kennedy I, p. 228-229.
5. *Ibid.*
6. Richmond *Enquirer,* 1808 quoted in Kennedy I, p. 230-242.
7. *Ibid.*
8. Kennedy I, p. 242-243.
9. Wirt to James Monroe, February 8, 1808, in Kennedy I, p. 250-253.
10. Wirt to Elizabeth Wirt, April 11, 1808, in Kennedy I, p. 249-250.
11. Kennedy I, p. 259-260.
12. *The Enquirer*, Richmond, January 31, 1909, cited in Robert, WWV, p. 416.
13. Robert, WWV, p. 416-417.
14. Wirt to Carr, p. 281-282.

Chapter 11: The 'Old Bachelor' Essays

1. Wirt to Benjamin Edwards, February 26, 1809, in Kennedy I, p. 261-261.
2. Wirt to Benjamin Edwards, June 23, 1809, in Kennedy I, p. 264-268.
3. Wirt to Benjamin Edwards, December 22, 1809, in Kennedy I, p. 273.
4. Kennedy I, p. 275-277.
5. Wirt to Thomas Jefferson, January 18, 1810, in Kennedy I, p. 278-279.
6. Kennedy I, p. 288-293.
7. William Wirt, *The Old Bachelor,* 3rd edition, Vol 1, (Baltimore, 1919), p. 5-6.
8. *Ibid*, p. 162.
9. *Ibid*, p. 202.
10. Wirt to Dabney Carr, quoted in Kennedy I, p. 292-293.
11. Davis, p. 283-284.
12. Wirt to Carr, February 15, 1811, quoted in Kennedy I, p. 293-305.
13. Davis, p. 284.
14. Wirt to St. George Tucker, February 25, 1815, St. George Tucker Collection, Manuscripts and Rare Books Dept., Earl Gregg Swem Library, College of William & Mary.
15. *Ibid*, p. 247, Kennedy I, p. 350.
16. Kennedy I, p. 348.

Chapter 12: The Realities of War

1.Samuel Eliot Morison and Henry Steele Commager, *The Growth of the American Republic*, vol. I, (N.Y., 1962), p. 399-419. Hereafter referred to as Morison.

2. Kennedy I, p. 323-341.

3. Wirt to Pres, James Madison (undated), quoted in Kennedy I, page 335.

4. Wirt to Judge Dabney Carr, August 23, 1813, in Kennedy I, p. 357-358.

5. Wirt to John T. Lomax, July 7, 1814, quoted in Kennedy I, p. 373.

6. Wirt to Elizabeth Wirt, Sept. 9-28, 1814, quoted in Kennedy I, p. 376-380.

7. Wirt to Elizabeth Wirt, October 14, 1814, quoted in Kennedy I, p. 380-382.

8. Wirt to Carr, Dec. 10, 1814, quoted in Kennedy I, p. 382.

Chapter 13: Before the Supreme Court

1. Wirt to Carr, December 10, 1814, quoted in Kennedy I, p. 382.

2. Wirt to Francis Gilmer, April 1, 1806, quoted in Kennedy I, p. 400-403.

3. *Ibid.*

4. Wirt to Carr (undated), quoted in Kennedy I, p. 404-407.

5. Wirt to James Madison, March 23, 1816, quoted in Kennedy I, p.398-400.

6. Minutes of Board of Trustees, College of New Jersey, vol. II (1797-1823), University Archives, Princeton University. Cited in Robert, WWV, p. 440.

7. Wirt to Carr, February 27, 1817, quoted in Kennedy II, p. 15.

8. *Ibid.*

9. *Ibid,* p. 16.

Chapter 14: 'A Life of Patrick Henry'

1. Kennedy II, p. 35-39.

2. *Ibid,* and Davis, p. 66.

3.John Adams to Wirt, January 5, 1818, quoted in Kennedy II, p.44-46.

4.Wirt to John Adams, January 12, 1818, quoted in Kennedy, II, p. 46-48.

5. Wirt to Carr, August 20, 1815, quoted in Kennedy I, p. 387-393.

6. Davis, p. 272.

7. David Arnold McCants, "The authenticity of William Wirt's version of Patrick Henry's 'liberty or death' speech," *Virginia Magazine of History & Biography*, vol. 87, no. 4 (Richmond, 1979), p.389-401.

8. St. George Tucker to Wirt, April 4, 1813, quoted in Kennedy I, p. 352-355.

9. Taylor, Wirt, p. 478.

10. William Wirt, *Sketches of the Life and Character of Patrick Henry*, (Ithaca, N.Y., 1847)., p. 92. Hereafter known as *Sketches.*

11. *Ibid,* p. 93-95.

12. Taylor, Wirt, p.478.

13. *Sketches,* p. 83, 87-88, 209.

14. Decius (probably a pseudonym for Maj. John Nicholas), *Decius' Letters,* pamphlet, 1818, quoted in Robert, WWV, p. 436.

15. Robert, Hon. Wirt, p. 54-55.

Chapter 15: Attorney General of the U.S.

1. Kennedy II, p. 55.

2. Kennedy II, p. 56.

3. Wirt to William Pope, January 18, 1818, quoted in Kennedy II, p. 66-71.

4. Wirt to Carr, January 21, 1818, quoted in Kennedy II, p. 73-75.

5. Samuel L. Southard, A Discourse on the Professional Character and Virtues of the Late William Wirt, (1834, Washington, D.C.).

6. Edward J. Cole, Reporter, *Trials of the Mail Robbers, Hare, Alexander and Hare,* (Baltimore, 1818) In Maryland Historical Society Collection, p. 10, 65, 92, 103, 186-195.

7. Wirt to Hugh Nelson, Chairman, House Judiciary Committee, March 27, 1818, quoted in Kennedy II, p. 61-65.

8. Samuel Southard, A Discourse on the Professional Character and Virtues of the Late William Wirt, (Washington, D.C., 1834). Also quoted in Kennedy I, p. 59-60.

9. Kennedy II, p. 59-60.

10. Wirt to Pope, January 18, 1818, quoted in Kennedy II, p. 70.

11. Wirt to Francis Gilmer, June 1, 1818, quoted in Kennedy II, p. 78.

12. Wirt to Pope, October 13, 1818, quoted in Kennedy II, p. 80-81.

13. Robert, "The Honorable William Wirt," *Supreme Court Yearbook*, 1976, p. 53. Hereafter known as Robert, *Hon. Wirt.*

Chapter 16: Wirt and the Marshall Court

1. Morison, p. 434-436.

2. *Ibid.*

3. *Ibid*, p. 434-436.

4. Webster to Wirt, p. 90-91, quoted in Kennedy II.

5. Robert, *Hon. Wirt*, p. 54.

6. Burke, p. 268.

7. Wirt argument, quoted in Kennedy II, p. 164-168.

8. Marshall opinion, quoted in Henry Steele Commager, ed., *Documents of American History,* (N.Y., 1948), p.238-242. Hereafter referred to as Commager, *Documents.*

9. Joseph Charles Burke, *William Wirt, Attorney General and Constitutional Lawyer* (Doctoral dissertation, University of Indiana, 1965), p. 75. Hereafter referred to as Burke.

Chapter 17: Counsel to Presidents

1. Robert Sobel (Ed.), *Biographical Dictionary of the United States Executive Branch, 1774-1977,* Greenwood Press (Westport, Ct., 1977),p. 410-411.

2. Robert, *Hon.Wirt,,* p. 52.

3. Kennedy II, p. 55-57.

4. Robert, *Hon. Wirt*, p. 56.

5. Dale Eisman, "Subpeona Case Opinion in 1818 Overlooked by Watergate Lawyers," *Richmond Times-Dispatch,* August 26, 1973. Hereafter referred to as Eisman.

6. *Ibid.*

7. Robert, *Hon. Wirt*, p. 56.

8. Eisman.

9. Burke, p.71.

10. *Ibid.*, p. 72.

11. *Ibid.*, p 73.

12. Charles Francis Adams, ed., *Memoirs of John Quincy Adams, Comprising Portions of His Diary from 1795-1848.* (New York, 1970), vol. IV, p. 83.

13. J. Monroe to John Adams, *Adams Family Papers*, Mass. Historical Society, in Noble E. Cunningham, *The Presidency of James Monroe.* U. of Kansas Press, 1966, p. 125. Hereafter known as Cunningham.

14. Adams Diary, Vol. 4, p. 112-119.

15. *National Intelligencer*, Washington, quoted in Cunningham, p. 61-62.

16. Adams Diary, Vol. 5, p. 5-12.
17. Adams Diary, Vol. 6, p. 195-210.
18. Charles Adams, ed., *John Quincy Adams Memoirs, Comprising Portions of his Diary from 1795-1848*. (Philadelphia, 1874-77.), vol. II, p. 58-64.
19. S.M. Hamilton, ed., *The Writings of James Monroe* (New York, 1893-1903), vol. II, p. 234-236.

Chapter 18: Wirt and Jefferson
1. Robert, WWV, p. 397.
2. *Ibid.*, p. 417.
3. *Ibid.*, p. 418.
4. *Ibid.*, p. 417-418.
5. Virginius Dabney, *Mr. Jefferson's University, A History*; (Charlottesville, 1981), p. 7. Hereafter referrred to as Dabney. (also Kennedy II, p. 207.)
6. Thomas Jefferson to Wirt, April 6, 1826, quoted in Kennedy II, p. 207-208.
7. Wirt to Thomas Jefferson, April 8, 1826, quoted in Kennedy II. p. 208-209.
8. Dabney, p. 7.
9. Kennedy II, p. 214-215.
10. Wirt to Pope, July 24, 1826, quoted in Kennedy II, p. 215-218.
11. Published text of Wirt's speech on death of Jefferson and Adams, Manuscript Section, Virginia Historical Society, Richmond.

Chapter 19: An Inspiration to Youth
1. Kennedy I, p. 324-326.
2. Gilmer Family File, Albemarle County Historical Society, Charlottesville.
3. Wirt to Francis Gilmer, July 23, 1815, quoted in Kennedy I, p. 385-386.
4. *Ibid,* September, 1815, quoted in Kennedy I, p. 386-389.
5. Kennedy II, p. 71-72.
6. Robert, *Hon. Wirt*, p. 52.
7. Wirt to T. Wallis, August 25, 1833, quoted in Kennedy II, p. 409-413.
8. Wirt to W. Miller, Dec. 20, 1833, quoted in Kennedy II, p. 414-420.
9. Charles H. Bohner, *John Pendleton Kennedy, Gentleman from Baltimore,* (Johns Hopkins Press, Baltimore, 1961). p. 52-59, 65, 81, 84.
10. Harvey Allen, *Israfel, The Life and of Edgar Allan Poe,* cited in Hubbell, Familiar Essay.
11. Dan and Inez Morris, *Who Was Who in American Politics*, (New York, 1974), p 145.
12. William Wirt, published *1830 Address to the Peithessophian and Philoclean Societies of Rutgers College,* Manuscript Section, Virginia Historical Society. Also quoted in Kennedy II.

Chapter 20: An End to an Era
1. James Monroe to Wirt, October 24, 1828, quoted in Kennedy II, p. 256-257.
2. Wirt to Carr, February 28, 1829, quoted in Kennedy II, p. 261-262.
3. Wirt to Pope, March 22, 1829, quoted in Kennedy II, p. 263-265.
4. Wirt to Cabell, June 14, 1829, quoted in Kennedy II, p.268-269.
5. Wirt to Carr, August 3, 1829, quoted in Kennedy II, p. 272-275.
6. Kennedy II, p. 308-329.
7. *Ibid.*
8. *Ibid.*

Chapter 21: The Cherokee Cases

1. Michael Oberg, "Wirt and the Trials of Republicanism," *Virginia Magazine of History and Biography, vol. 87, 1979,* Virginia Historical Society, Richmond, p. 311-317. Hereafter referred to as Oberg.
2. *Ibid.*
3. Marquis James, *Andrew Jackson, Portrait of a President,* (New York, 1937), p. 246.
4. William Wirt, published arguments in *Cherokee Nation v. Georgia* (copy at Virginia Historical Society.)
5. *Ibid.*
6. *Ibid.*
7. *Ibid.*
8. Burke, p. 255-257.
9. Burke, p. 255-257. Commager, *Documents,* p. 258-261.
10. Commager, *Documents,* p. 259.
11. Samuel Eliot Morison and Henry Steele Commager, *The Growth of the American Republic,* vol. 1, Oxford U. Press (New York, 1962), p. 489.
12. Conmmager, *Documents,* p. 258-262.
13. Oberg, p.317.

Chapter 22: Wirt for President

1. Wirt to Carr, May 22, 1831, quoted in Kennedy II, p. 346.
2. Samuel Rhea Gammon Jr., *The Presidential Campaign of 1832,* doctoral dissertation, Johns Hopkins University (Baltimore, 1922), p. 33-52. Hereafter referred to as Gammon.
3. Wirt to delegates of Anti-Mason Party, September 28, 1831, quoted in Kennedy II, p. 352-356.
4. *Ibid.*
5. Wirt to Carr, September 30, 1831, quoted in Kennedy II, p. 356-358.
6. Wirt to Salmon P. Chase, November 11, 1831, in Kennedy II, p. 356- 361.
7. Kennedy II, p. 361-362.
8. Gammon, p. 68.
9. Wirt to Carr, December 5, 1831, quoted in Kennedy, 362-364.
10. *Ibid.*
11. Wirt to Carr, January 12, 1832, quoted in Kennedy II, p.362-369.
12. Wirt to Carr, October 25, 1832, quoted in Kennedy II, p. 378-380.
13. Oberg, p. 320.
14. Wirt to Judge T. Randall, July 29, 1833, quoted in Kennedy II, p. 398-399.

Chapter 23: The Clock Runs Down

1. Wirt to Rev. John Rice, February 1, 1822, quoted in Kennedy II, p. 135-137.
2. Wirt to Francis Gilmer, May 9, 1822, quoted in Kennedy II, p. 137-139.
3. Wirt to Dabney Carr, August 9, 1817, William Wirt Papers, University of North Carolina, quoted in Robert, WWV, p. 425.
4. Robert, *Hon. Wirt,* p. 55.
5. Wirt memoir, quoted in Kennedy II, p. 331-334.
6. Wirt to Judge Randall, March 8, 1833, quoted in Kennedy II, p. 393-394.
7. Wirt to S. T. Wallis, August 25, 1833, quoted in Kennedy II, p. 393-394.
8. Wirt to Carr, December 25, 1833, quoted in Kennedy II, p. 421-422.
9. Wirt to Judge Cabell, Christmas, 1833, quoted in Kennedy II, p. 422-423.
10. Wirt to Judge Randall, Christmas, 1833, quoted in Kennedy II, p. 421.
11. Wirt to Judge Cabell, January 4, 1834, quoted in Kennedy II, p. 423.

Chapter 24: The Florida Fling

1. William H. Gaines Jr., "Guns, Silkworms and Pigs, Bellona Arsenal and Bellona Foundry," *The Virginia Cavalcade,* vol. III, no. 2, Autumn, 1953, p. 32-37.
2. Jerrell H. Shofner, *History of Jefferson County,* Sentry Press (Tallahassee, 1976), p. 85-89. Hereafter cited as Shofner.
3. Wirt to Randall, January 29, 1833, quoted in Kennedy II, p. 387- 389; Wirt to Elizabeth Wirt, January 31, 1833, quoted in Kennedy II, p. 387-389.
4. Wirt to Louis Goldsborough, Feb. 2, 1833, quoted in Kennedy II, p. 390-392.
5. Wirt to Randall, March 22, 1833, quoted in Kennedy II, p. 394.
6. Wirt to Goldsborough, March 30, 1833, quoted in Kennedy II, p. 394-395.
7. Wirt to Goldsborough, April 30, 1833, quoted in Kennedy, II, p. 396.
8. Wirt to Goldsborough, July 18, 1833, quoted in Kennedy II, p. 398.
9. Randall to Wirt, Sept. 29, 1833, Wirt Papers, MHS, quoted in Shofner, p. 91.
10. Wirt to Randall, July 29, 1833, quoted in Kennedy II, p. 398.
11. *Webster's New Biographical Dictionary,* (Springfield, Mass., 1983), p. 408.
12. Randall to Wirt, January 22, November 19 & 27, 1932, and February, 1833, Wirt Papers, quoted in Shofner.
13. A.J. Hanna, *A Prince in their Midst, The Adventurous Life of Achille Murat on the American Frontier,* University of Oklahoma Press (Norman, 1946), p. 7-13, 25, 110-128.
14. Shofner, p. 93-94.

Chapter 25: The End

1. Kennedy II, p. 423-425.
2. Robert, *Hon. Wirt,* p. 51. Also Robert WWV., p. 388.
3. Kennedy II, p. 425-426.
4. *Ibid.*
5. *Ibid.,* p. 427.
6. *Ibid.,* p. 427-428.
7. *Ibid.,* p. 428-429.
8. The Norfolk *American Beacon,* February 22, 1834, (Microfilm, Kirn Memorial Library, Norfolk.)
9. R.B. Davis, p. 385-386.
10. Telephone Interview with Prof. Bernie Allen, West Virginia University at Parkersburg.
11. George W. Sherwood, Eulogy on the Life and Character of William Wirt, (Baltimore, 1834), p31-32
12. Robert, 1972 Speech on bicentennial of William Wirt's birth, original manuscript at Virginia Historical Society, Richmond.

Index